THE PLAIN ENGLISH APPROACH TO
BUSINESS WRITING

The Plain English Approach to Business Writing

EDWARD P. BAILEY, JR.

New York   Oxford
OXFORD UNIVERSITY PRESS
1990

11-90

21080839

For my wife, Janet,
and daughters, Laura and Jeannette

Oxford University Press

Oxford   New York   Toronto
Delhi   Bombay   Calcutta   Madras   Karachi
Petaling Jaya   Singapore   Hong Kong   Tokyo
Nairobi   Dar es Salaam   Cape Town
Melbourne   Auckland

and associated companies in
Berlin   Ibadan

Published by Oxford University Press, Inc.
200 Madison Avenue, New York, NY 10016

Library of Congress Cataloging-in-Publication Data
Bailey, Edward P.
The plain English approach to business writing
Edward P. Bailey, Jr.
p. cm.   ISBN 0-19-506490-9
1. Business writing.   I. Title.
HF5718.3.B35   1990
808'.06665—dc20   90-31277

2 4 6 8 9 7 5 3 1

Printed in the United States of America
on acid free paper

Acknowledgments

Through the years, I've become indebted to others for what I know about plain English. Two people, in particular, stand out: Rudolf Flesch and Dr. Tom Murawski.

I never personally met Rudolf Flesch, a pioneer in plain English, but I did meet him through his writing. His books are masterpieces of conciseness and good advice, as clear and sparkling today as they were years ago. I wish I had met him while he lived.

The other person who stands out is Tom Murawski. Fifteen years ago, while I still wrote "bureaucratese," Tom handed me a book by Rudolf Flesch and said, "Ed, you need to read this." I wondered why—but found out as soon as I'd read the first few pages. Tom has been my friend, colleague, associate for all these years. His intense interest in plain English inspired me at the beginning; his continual insights and genius have kept me inspired ever since.

Others have contributed, too, and I wish to take an author's privilege to acknowledge them here:

- Judy Clark and Mary Anne Weaver, my friends, for the help they have given me throughout the years at the National Defense University.
- Phil Powell—longstanding friend, co-author on three

books, and "world-class" editor—for the polish he's added to the writing of hundreds of people (including me).

- General Bradley Hosmer, Rhodes Scholar and military leader, who understands the written word and values its importance.
- Dr. Fred Kiley, quintessential teacher, who helped me get going as a college professor and keeps me on the right path today.
- Dr. Robert Sigethy and Dr. Joan Feeney, colleagues at Marymount University, whose professionalism I admire tremendously.
- Dr. Jim Gaston, close friend and colleague over the years, who has shared the love of writing and teaching with me.

My thanks also to Bill Klein, who provided one of the samples of good writing that I use, and to the reviewers whose comments helped shape the book: Susan Leatherwood, Jeannette Bailey, and Janet Hiller.

Finally, of course, my appreciation to my editor at Oxford University Press: Bill Sisler. I am indeed fortunate to have worked with Oxford and with him.

Arlington, Virginia   E.P.B.
January 1990

Contents

THE NEW WAY
TO WRITE

CHAPTER 1

What Is Plain English?

Pointing to the second paragraph of a report, my friend said, "Right about here my mind gets a little bit fuzzy. I see these reports every day, but I put off reading them as long as possible. Sometimes," he admitted, "I don't read them at all."

We've all been there, haven't we? We've all struggled with somebody else's writing, trying to make sense of it because that's what we're paid to do. Do you know that the fault—the reason we have to struggle—is almost always not ours? Instead, the fault is almost always the writer's!

I learned that lesson the hard way, partly as the reader who was having trouble, but mainly as the writer who was causing it. For, I must admit, I'm a reformed bad writer.

This book will tell you the lessons I've learned along the way, lessons that have made writing much easier for me to do, and (I hope) much easier for others to read. It should help you, and the people who work for you, write more easily and clearly, too. For this is a book on plain English.

A Reformed Bad Writer . . .

Ironically, when I discovered plain English, I was teaching writing in college. You can guess what I had been teaching: an overly formal style designed more to impress than simply to communicate clearly to the reader.

Since then, I've switched to plain English and taught it extensively—in college, and to thousands of people in government and business. This book is a result of those experiences, and it's designed to help you discover plain English—not just as a reader, but as a *writer*, too.

When you make that discovery, you will find that writing is much easier for you—and it will be better, too.

What Is Plain English—And What Isn't?

Let's start with what *isn't* plain English. Businessese isn't plain English, nor is academese, bureaucratese, legalese, or any other "-ese." Here's an example of some businessese from a federal regulation:

Businessese

Each application shall be supported by a comprehensive letter of explanation in duplicate. This letter shall set forth all the facts required to present to this office a complete disclosure of the transaction.

Those of you with business experience know that passage is just beginning businessese, relatively uncomplicated compared to what the true Masters of Gobbledygook can turn out.

Nevertheless, it could be more straightforward. Here's a better version, losing absolutely no preciseness:

Plain English

You must send us the following:

- one copy of your application
- two copies of a letter explaining the complete details of your transaction

---

See the difference? You can understand the first version with a little effort, but you'd hate to read several paragraphs—or pages—in that style. The second version won't win the Nobel prize for literature, but it *is* straightforward communication.

And, at times, plain English does approach art. A clean, straightforward document can be beautiful in its simplicity and efficiency.

Why Is Plain English Better Than the "Other Way"?

I've already mentioned the two chief reasons for writing plain English:

- It's far easier for your reader to read.
- It's far easier for you to write.

You don't need many more advantages than those, do you? But let's look further.

In the past, plain English seemed merely a preference: you like the old way, and I like plain English. Who's to decide? Well, psycholinguists have made the decision easier. Their work shows clearly that plain English is easier for all of us to read, *no matter how smart we are*. And, as you might expect, the typical bureaucratic style is *harder* for all of us to read—also, no matter how smart we are.

For example, psycholinguists have learned that we all take

longer to read less familiar words (like *commence*) than familiar ones (like *begin*). The difference is only a few hundred milliseconds in time—but a lot less strain on the short-term memory (and the older I get, the less strain I want to put on mine). The implication? As writers, we can help our readers by preferring ordinary words.

That's just one very brief example of what the psycholinguists have been up to. I investigated their study at length in another book, *Writing Clearly: A Contemporary Approach*.

Because of the work of the psycholinguists, writing style is no longer like the width of lapels: "What's the style this year—wide or narrow?" Instead, there's solid scientific underpinning for the plain English movement.

There's a further reason for writing plain English, too: the impact on the boss.

Suppose *you're* the boss—a manager with 15 people working for you. A prestigious project comes in, requiring a report. Only two of your people are both qualified to work on it and reasonably available. One has a straightforward style that's easy for you and your client to understand. The other writes with a complex bureaucratic style that makes you reach for the aspirin bottle.

Who will you choose?

If you assign the project to the bad writer, you know you'll have to do extensive rewriting (and maybe most of the *writing*, too). On the other hand, if you assign the project to the good writer, you can do what you're paid to do: manage. And the final product will be much better because you can spend your time evaluating drafts for content instead of struggling simply to decipher them.

Who Is Writing Plain English These Days?

Sad to say, many people today still write businessese. But many have also shifted to plain English. In other words, there's a "fence"—with some people on the bureaucratic side and others on the plain English side.

Fortunately, more and more people are moving to the plain English side—and when people reach that side, they never jump back. The advantages of plain English are just too obvious.

Also, many large organizations today are endorsing plain English:

- *Private Business.* Many successful companies require plain English—especially for writing going outside the company. Major improvement in writing has occurred in the fields of insurance, computers, banking, and health care.
- *Federal Agencies.* Many (perhaps *most*) top federal agencies are training their people to write in plain English—such agencies as the Department of Commerce, the Federal Energy Regulatory Commission, the Internal Revenue Service, and the U. S. Marshals Service.
- *U. S. Military.* Each military service strongly urges plain English—by regulation (and those regulations are in plain English, too).

The move today is clearly toward plain English because it works. This book will show you how to write it.

What Will You Learn in This Book?

There's a method to this book. The first four chapters take you through the basics of plain English. Chapter 5 then gives you a model that will work for much business writing. This model helps you get started writing and makes sure that your organization will be easy to follow.

The model is easy to understand and use, and it can apply to anything from simple memos to complex, highly technical reports. I've used it myself many times to help top organizations simplify their writing. The beauty of the model is that it works! Beginning with Chapter 6, you'll learn how to add polish to

the basics. The table of contents shows you the book's chapters.
Here are the book's key topics:

- *Style*. How can you write sentences that are clear, precise,
easy on your readers?
- *Organization*. How can you be sure your readers always
know where they are and what your point is?
- *Layout*. How can you show your readers—visually—what
your organization is?
- *Punctuation*. How can you gain emphasis by using the
"other" marks of punctuation: the colon, dash, question
mark, and semicolon?
- *Abstractness*. How can you avoid this killer of plain English
by using details and examples to make your point?
- *Passive Voice*. How can you avoid this second killer of plain
English—passive voice? And just what is passive voice,
anyway?
- *The Writing Process*. What's the easiest way to get words on
paper? What role does the computer play in that process?
- *Supervising Writers*. As a supervisor, what can you do to get
the best writing from your people?

So let's begin the journey. For many, it has changed their lives.
I know it has changed mine.

CHAPTER 2

Style: Writing a Readable Sentence

Let's start with a quiz. Choose "a" or "b":

A Quiz

1. How have you *produced* most of the words in your life?
   a. by writing them
   b. by speaking them
2. How have you *received* most of the words in your life?
   a. by reading them
   b. by hearing them

For most of us, the answers are both "b": we've *spoken* many more words than we've written, and we've *heard* many more than we've read. The language we're most used to, then, is spoken English.

"What does that have to do with writing?" you may ask.

Everything. You see, in bureaucratic writing, words and sentences are far different from those of spoken English. But in plain English, words and sentences are more like those in spoken English. Spoken English is the language we're most comfortable with—the language that works for us.

9

That's why most professional writers use spoken English when they write. Check the editorial section of your newspaper. What do you find there? If your paper is typical, you'll find the editors use spoken English. Look in one of the most popular papers in the world: *The Wall Street Journal.* You'll certainly find spoken English there.

In fact, the biggest headline on page 1 of every *Wall Street Journal* is "What's News—." The contraction makes the tone informal, and the dash leads the reader into the text that follows. Informal tone and awareness of the reader are two common characteristics of spoken—and plain—English.

The Key Advice: "Write the Way You Talk"

Thus, the key to plain English is this: Talk to your reader. Simply talk on paper. Write the way you talk.

Imagine you're actually standing in front of your reader. Or talking on the telephone. What would you say—in an organized and polite way? Then write those words.

Sound simplistic? Some people are afraid that "writing the way you talk" means being simple-minded, writing like a kindergartner. But that would be true only if you talk like a kindergartner. The advice is to write the way *you* talk.

Let's look at some spoken English. Here's an excerpt by H. Ross Perot, a billionaire who wrote this editorial about the stock market crash in 1987. Notice how much like conversation the style is, and notice that the content is far from simple-minded:

From "A Tycoon Looks at the Debt Bomb"

I got out of the stock market about a year ago because I couldn't understand what was happening. The optimism of the market didn't fit with the problems in the economy. So I invested instead in short-term, high quality liquid securities—such as Treasury bills and high-grade bonds. . . .

So let's take an honest look at our problems at the end of this topsy-turvy week on Wall Street. What forces caused the dramatic ups and downs in the stock market, sending economic signals flashing like the fire-warning lights on an aircraft instrument panel? Here are some of them:

- Our country, effectively, does not have a budget. We avoid facing the budget issue by passing continuing resolutions that put us deeper into debt each year. . . .
- Our principal exports from New York harbor are scrap steel and waste paper to Japan. These materials are shipped back to America as automobiles and corrugated cardboard boxes containing sophisticated consumer electronics. It is hard to believe that the greatest nation in the world could be reduced to becoming a scrap salesman—but it's happening.

We Americans have evolved from a tough, resilient people, willing to sacrifice for future generations, into a people who want to feel good now—at any price—and let the future take care of itself. Put more directly, we have become credit junkies, shooting up huge sums of borrowed money on a government and personal level—looking for another high.

Doesn't Perot sound as if he's simply talking to us? And although he's using ordinary words, he's not expressing ordinary ideas. There's nothing "kindergarten" about this article.

So just *look* for spoken English: look in magazines, newspapers, successful books. And *listen* for it, too: listen to the most moving speeches, the best newscasts.

What you will find is that the best of writing and the best of speaking have much in common. And what they have in common produces plain English.

Should We *Really* Write the Way We Talk?

Well . . . we don't want to write the way we sometimes talk, complete with the occasional "uhs" and rambling, disconnected sentences. But if you imagine a reader in front of you, if you imagine you are actually talking on paper to that reader, the words will come out like the best of speaking—and the best of writing, too.

When I write, I believe I am actually putting down the words as I would say them to you. I sit in front of a computer, "talking" to my imaginary reader.

So don't worry about the theoretical differences between writing and speaking. Simply talk on paper. Talk to your reader.

Specific Tips for Writing the Way You Talk

To talk on paper, you may have to change your writing. For example, when you write:

- Do you normally use words like *commence* instead of *begin*, and *prior to* instead of *before*?
- Do you normally avoid all marks of punctuation except the period and the comma?
- Do you normally avoid using any personal pronouns—like *I*, *we*, and *you*?

If so, you're a typical bureaucratic writer. Get ready to make the most important step in your writing career. Here's what I suggest:

- Use ordinary words.
- Use a variety of punctuation.
- Use more personal pronouns.
- Use contractions (sometimes).

If you're like me before I began writing plain English, these suggestions probably seem like heresy, like crimes against the

English language. Now, though, I think I committed my crimes before I followed these suggestions—not after.

Let's examine those four suggestions in more detail.

Use Ordinary Words

Look over this list:

Simpler Words and Phrases

Bureaucratic	Ordinary
accompany	go with
advise	tell
assist	help
at the present time	now
close proximity	near
commence	begin
complete	fill out
endeavor	try
forward	send
herewith is	here is
indicate	show, tell

Which column do you normally choose your words from when you're writing?

If you're the way I used to be, you probably choose from the left-hand side. In fact, when I first saw a list like this, I was shocked to find that I chose *most* of my words from the left-hand side. And I could have given you very good reasons, too—something to do with nuances of meaning.

Then I noticed I consistently used words from the *right-hand* side when I spoke. Why were the nuances so important when I wrote but not when I talked? After serious soul searching, I realized that the so-called nuances weren't really there at all. Instead, I had come to believe that I needed to write with a formal tone—that was the real reason I was choosing the more "impressive" words. As a result, I'd stopped writing with my most important vocabulary: the words I use in speaking each day.

So here's my advice on words. Do as the good professionals do:

- Good professionals use *ordinary* words unless they need something more precise—which happens all the time.
- But bad amateurs use *impressive* words all the time—unless they can't think of them.

To see what I mean, let's look at writing by a successful professional, Russell Baker. This is the first paragraph of one of his books, *Growing Up* (which won the Pulitzer Prize). He's telling us about his mother, who's in a nursing home but doesn't realize she's there. She's living in the past.

As you read, notice that the passage says *extraordinary* things with *ordinary* words:

From *Growing Up* by Russell Baker

At the age of eighty my mother had her last bad fall, and after that her mind wandered free through time. Some days she went to weddings and funerals that had taken place half a century earlier. On others she presided over family dinners cooked on Sunday afternoons for children who were now gray with age. Through all this, she lay in bed but moved across time, traveling among the dead decades with a speed and an ease beyond the gift of physical science.

Nice, isn't it? And where are the "impressive" words? About the only one is *presided*—a good choice that gives us the sense of the matriarch, the woman in control. As I said, such choices help with preciseness.

But ordinary words are precise, too. Do any of Baker's phrases stand out as especially well chosen? I like "her mind wandered free through time." Where's the "impressive" word there? There isn't one—yet the idea is far from ordinary or simple. And preciseness? The word "wandered"—a perfectly plain word—is right on target.

Writing with ordinary words doesn't mean writing with kindergarten language or producing only simple-minded ideas.

Writing with "impressive" words does mean making the reader's job harder. Even though we know all the words in the left-hand column, we have more trouble reading them, particularly if many appear in the same sentence or paragraph. And they usually do if writers consistently choose their words from the left-hand side.

For example, let's look at a sentence with mainly "impressive" words:

Using "Impressive Words"

Subsequent to the passage of subject legislation, it is incumbent upon you to advise your organization to comply with it.

And if we rewrite that sentence with ordinary words:

Using Ordinary Words

After the law passes, you must tell your people to comply with it.

Would you rather read pages of the first version or the second?

By the way, the second version keeps the phrase "comply with it." It could have said something like "follow it," but the word *comply* seems to make the message a little more urgent. So I don't suggest you always choose the ordinary word. But—to use a word from computer terminology—make ordinary words your *default*. Choose other words if preciseness demands, just as you do when you speak.

And ask yourself what words Russell Baker (the professional who wrote about his mother) would choose if he were writing your document.

For a list of simpler words and phrases, see the Appendix.

Use a Variety of Punctuation

The second suggestion on style is to use a variety of punctuation. Too often business writers use only periods and commas.

Have you ever heard anybody speak in a monotone? Well, people who write with only periods and commas are like speakers who speak in a monotone, forcing you—the audience—to do too much work: "What was important in that sentence? What's going to be carried over to the next sentence?" The audience has to figure that out because the speaker, using a monotone, isn't helping.

Good speakers do help, though. They use hand gestures and voice inflection to help their listeners along. Good writers, using spoken English, allow punctuation to replace those hand gestures and that voice inflection.

This chapter doesn't cover all the important marks of punctuation you need to learn. Chapter 6 does that. But this chapter does look at one easy punctuation mark—the question—to illustrate the need for more than periods and commas.

A number of years ago, someone asked if I ever used questions in my writing. I realized that I never did, and I didn't know why. So let me ask you now: "Do you use questions in your writing? If you look at the last 10 pages you've written, will you find any?"

If your answer is "yes," you know one of the secrets of effective writing. Let's look more closely at why.

We all would have trouble talking without questions, real questions that ask for answers:

- When does the new copying machine get here?
- How far is Santa Fe from Albuquerque?

Those requests for information are fine in writing.

But let's focus now on another kind of question, one that packs much more power: the question that you, the *writer*, will answer. Such questions focus what you're saying and emphasize your answer—just as vocal inflection and hand gestures do when you're talking. In other words, such questions draw the reader in.

Let's look at an example. Here's some writing in a monotone (without questions):

Without Questions

The main point is that the defective computer disks are not the responsibility of the manufacturer, as we first suspected, but of the wholesaler, who stored them at a 130 degree temperature.

Now let's add questions:

With Questions

Just who is responsible for the defective computer disks? Is it the manufacturer, as we first suspected? Not at all: the defective disks are the responsibility of the <u>wholesaler</u>—who stored them at a <u>130 degree</u> temperature.

See the difference questions make?

Yes, there's also a dash, a colon, and underlining in the second passage. And that's the real message: use a variety of punctuation to control your emphasis and replace the hand gestures and voice inflection we all use in speaking.

The question mark is one easy way to start. Chapter 6 will tell you about the colon, the dash, and the semicolon.

Use More Personal Pronouns

Now for an even more important question: "Do you ever use personal pronouns in your writing?" In some audiences I speak to, about half the people say yes. In others, almost everyone uses them. In still other audiences, almost no one.

Here are the important pronouns for plain English:

Important Pronouns for Plain English

First Person: I, me, my, mine, we, us, our, ours

Second Person: you, your, yours

Many of us learned at some time not to use these personal pronouns. That idea comes partly from the outdated notion that important business writing must be formal. Yet the notion of what makes good writing is changing, and a more personal, informal tone is gaining wide acceptance for all kinds of writing.

Another reason people write without personal pronouns is to seem more objective—as though removing pronouns (especially first person) somehow removes all human fallibility. I remember asking one of the top executives in a federal agency what he felt about first person. The conversation went like this:

ME: "Some of your people feel they shouldn't use first person—*I, me, we*—in their writing because they'd seem to be giving their opinions. What do you think?"

HIM: "I *hire* people for their opinions! Personal pronouns are an *excellent* way for them to express their opinions—to me and to anyone else."

Don't most bosses hire people for the judgment they can exercise—in other words, for their opinions?

Not too long ago, some organizations even objected to the second person pronoun, *you*. For example, can you imagine reading a book telling how to do something if the book never uses the pronoun *you*? The early computer manuals did just that:

Computer Manual—Old-Style

The disk must first be placed in the A-drive and then the computer must be turned on. A menu with the . . .

The computer industry learned that manuals need to be user friendly. And user friendly means talking on paper to the users. Now you're more likely to find a computer manual saying this:

Computer Manual—User Friendly

First, put the disk in the A-drive. Then turn the computer on. You'll then see a menu with . . .

The differences in these two short samples are few, but users of entire computer manuals certainly noted the change in approach (and so did the writers of those manuals and the sellers of computers and computer products!).

One reason for using pronouns is that you will more likely use active—instead of passive—voice. The passage from the old-style computer manual, for example, uses passive voice for both verbs: *be placed* and *be turned on*. Chapter 10 discusses passive voice in detail, but you've certainly heard of its bad reputation. That reputation is well deserved: passive sentences are usually harder to read, especially if the content is complex or if several of them appear in a row.

So one reason to use personal pronouns is that your sentences will more likely be in active voice and, thus, easier to read.

Another reason to use pronouns is that you can *write* more easily with them. Can you imagine talking without ever using personal pronouns? I try that experiment during my classes, giving a volunteer a topic and then asking the person to tell us about it without using *I*, *me*, *you*, and so forth. The volunteer immediately becomes uncomfortable, stays silent a few seconds, and then begins with something like this: "Uh."

Without exception, the volunteers say that trying to talk without personal pronouns is extremely difficult. They also report that when they do find words to speak, those words usually express different ideas—not what the volunteers wanted to say in the first place but only what they could say. In other words, not only was communication harder, but the content changed to meet the artificial requirement of not using the pronouns.

In business, how often do you want your people to alter their content to meet the same artificial requirement?

When we try to write without using personal pronouns—as many people do—we have to put a "mental editor" between our thoughts and the page (or computer screen). That mental editor tries desperately to strip out personal pronouns and restate the ideas without them. Writing with that mental editor is hard work. And, as most professional writers have discovered, it's unnecessary, too.

So the next time you write, talk on paper, and let the personal pronouns come naturally.

Must you always use pronouns to be a good writer? No. Some writing—just like some speaking—simply doesn't call for them. For example, if you're describing a disk drive (instead of telling how to use it), you probably won't need personal pronouns at all: "A disk drive has three major components: the housing mechanism, the drive head, and the . . . ").

So the key isn't really to use personal pronouns: the key is to stop avoiding them. You don't try to *use* pronouns when you're talking, but you certainly don't try to *avoid* them, either, do you? Use the same system for your writing.

That's why most news reporting doesn't include personal pronouns: it's like describing the disk drive. It simply doesn't tempt the reporter to use pronouns in writing or speaking. But editorial writing more often does include them—especially the editorial *we*.

So get rid of that tyrannical mental editor. Start *"un*avoiding" a few pronouns!

Use Contractions (Sometimes)

What about contractions? Must you use them to write plain English? Surprisingly, no.

Contractions do nothing for readability. If you take writing with contractions in it and simply *"un*contract"—that is, change *can't* to *cannot* and *don't* to *do not*—the writing won't be any harder to read.

There will be a difference, though: the tone will seem more formal, more distant, without contractions. Is that a problem? Not necessarily. With matters of *readability*, there usually is a definite right and wrong—easier to read is better, everything else being equal. With matters of *tone*, though, there isn't a definite right or wrong—only what's appropriate for the situation.

Do you want to seem close to your reader (for friendly or unfriendly purposes)? Then use contractions (*The Wall Street Journal* does). Do you want objective distance? Then write without contractions. The readability will be the same; the tone will be different.

So if you always use contractions when you write, you're probably making a mistake. And if you never use them, you are also probably making a mistake—at least some of the time.

All that said, the problem with most business writing isn't *underusing* contractions. You see, although contractions don't affect *readability*, they do affect *write-ability*. That is, you are much more likely to write plain English if you use contractions.

For example, I helped a large federal agency rewrite one of its most important regulations. We decided we wanted the tone to remain formal and objective, so we chose not to use contractions in the final version. But we wrote the drafts using contractions.

Why? Because when people who weren't used to writing plain English tried writing without contractions, their writing returned to typical legalese. They stopped talking on paper. When we began writing drafts with contractions, the writing improved. Then, after writing with contractions, we simply "*un*contracted" later (with help from our computers). The result was plain English with a formal tone.

So I strongly urge you to use contractions when you write your drafts. Then *un*contract when necessary. *If* necessary.

What About the Rules We Learned in School?

At this point, you may be wondering if we should pay attention to anything we learned in school. That depends on the school, because many are terrific. But we all need to follow certain rules or else communication will become hopelessly erratic.

There are three categories of rules to consider:

- rules we all agree with
- rules few people agree with
- rules amateurs follow and professionals don't

Let's look more closely at each of these.

Rules We All Agree With

Some rules just aren't controversial. For example, we all know to start sentences with capital letters and end them with periods or other terminal marks of punctuation. We also want subjects to agree with verbs, and pronouns to agree with the nouns they replace.

There aren't really a lot of these rules that cause us a problem. For the most part, people in business know them and follow them.

Rules Few People Agree With

There's another category of rules "experts" on language try to foist on us. Jim Quinn, author of *American Tongue and Cheek*, calls these "experts" pop grammarians—people who seem to have a stone tablet from God filled with "The Commandments" on usage.

One of those pop grammarians, according to Quinn, is Edwin Newman, author of *Strictly Speaking*. In *Strictly Speaking*, Newman is appalled by the construction *convince to* (as in "The Soviet Union evidently is not able to *convince* Cairo *to* accept a rapid cease-fire."). In all my teaching and consulting, I've never found another soul who agrees with Newman on that issue. Yet he calls it "one of the worst things" *The New York Times* does.

Don't worry about the pop grammarians. They're talking—and mainly arguing—only with each other. Virtually all linguists, the real experts on language, disagree with the pop grammarians.

Rules Amateurs Follow and Professionals Don't

Professionals *are* professionals because readers pay for what they write. (How much would you pay for the stuff in your "in" box?) Professionals follow the standard rules (such as beginning sentences with capital letters); they ignore almost all of the rules by the pop grammarians; and they ignore a few rules they learned in school.

What are the rules from school the professionals have learned to ignore? John Trimble, in his classic book *Writing with Style: Conversations on the Art of Writing*, lists "The Seven Nevers":

The Seven Nevers

1. Never begin a sentence with *and* or *but*.
2. Never use contractions.
3. Never refer to the reader as *you*.
4. Never use the first person pronoun *I*.
5. Never end a sentence with a preposition.
6. Never split an infinitive.
7. Never write a paragraph containing only a single sentence.

Trimble then says he's going to "wrestle with the Nevers in the manner of an exorcist with unholy demons, earnestly hoping that I may free you of their hold forever."

I agree. The Seven Nevers would be good rules only if we make a key revision. You guessed it: strike out the word *never*! That's what almost all professionals have learned to do. Again, just look at professional writing, and you'll see you've been reading spoken English—plain English—complete with split infinitives, one-sentence paragraphs, and sentences ending with prepositions. Just the way we talk.

So remember the most important lesson on style: write the way you talk! It's much easier—on your reader and on you.

CHAPTER 3

Organization:
Getting to the Point

The key advice on organization is simple: start with your main point. Tell your readers, right at the start:

- what your conclusion will be
- or what you want them to do
- or whatever your main purpose is for your document

I'll cover two techniques for getting to the point: the *opening statement* and the *opening summary*.

The Opening Statement

An opening statement is simply a sentence or so at the beginning of a document that states your main point. It doesn't have to be the first sentence (although it could be), but it should be way up front—usually in the first paragraph.

Why is an opening statement important? Put yourself in the place of a reader. What do you do if you're reading a 10-page document that has the main point buried near the end? Most of us just skip to the end.

We simply don't put up with writing that asks us to slog through fact, fact, fact, logic, logic, logic to reach that "perfect" bottom line. If the writer doesn't start with the bottom line, we—as readers—do. We make the bottom line the top line by skipping ahead. We take charge of the organization because the writer didn't.

Again, put yourself in the reader's position. Suppose you've just had outside auditors look over your financial records. They've spent 3 months with access to all your files and all your people. Today they hand you their report. Do you want to read all their facts—everything they examined—to find that your company looks great? Or that one of your division managers has been cheating? Wouldn't you rather have the conclusion up front?

For instance, consider these two good starts for audit reports (each with the bottom line up front):

Report of Audit: Two Good Beginnings

After 3 months of examining your records for the past year, we have found no major discrepancies.

or

After 3 months of examining your records for the past year, we have found the following:

- Your marketing division is systematically hiding its losses each month—totalling $300,000 for the past 6 months alone.
- The division manager and his assistant appear to be the only people involved.
- There were no other major discrepancies.

These two starts work better than delaying the conclusions until the end of a long report, don't they?

Notice that starting with the main point doesn't mean saying only what you're going to cover: "This report tells you the re-

sults of the audit we've been conducting for the past 3 months."
No, starting with the main point means telling what you found.
Starting with only the topic simply isn't enough—just as a table
of contents usually isn't enough to serve as the summary of a
book.

When Do We Want the Main Point Up Front?

Of course we want an auditor to tell us the bottom line first.
When else do we want to hear the bottom line right away? How
about these times:

- When we're reading a legal brief—just what is the lawyer's
  final opinion?
- When we're reading a doctor's report on our health—are
  we going to make it another year?
- When we're reading the results of a proposal to do some
  work for a client—did we win or not?
- When we're reading an employee's recommendation.
- When we get our budget for the next year.

The list could go on and on, couldn't it?
Now a shorter list: when do we want the main point at the
end?

- When we're reading a mystery story.

Is there any other time?
What about short documents—do we need the main point up
front then? That's not as crucial as for long reports, but even for
something short we appreciate getting the main point early. For
example, what if you're having a busy day as personnel director
for your company, and this comes in from an employment
agency:

Short Letter with the Main Point Buried

Dear Personnel Director:

On December 15, I received a phone call from Mr. Albert Rosnall from Utah, who was a mail clerk in your Denver office. Mr. Rosnall, who was under the direct supervision of Ms. Mary Allen, has requested I contact you. He requests a letter of verification of employment, including job title and duties he performed while in your office. According to Mr. Rosnall, he needs this in order to apply for a similar position in his new company.

I would appreciate your help in this matter.

Sincerely,

What's the key sentence buried in that letter? It's the one asking for the verification of employment. You can find it without experiencing major frustration, but wouldn't you have preferred the request first—like this:

Short Letter with the Main Point Up Front

Dear Personnel Director:

Would you verify the employment of Mr. Albert Rosnall?

Mr. Rosnall was a mail clerk in your Denver office [then give the rest of the details]. . . .

Sincerely,

Better, isn't it?

Why Don't People Routinely Begin with the Main Point?

If beginning with the main point is something readers clearly prefer, why don't more writers begin that way? Most writers don't think about it—they simply use the same order on paper in which events actually occurred. I'm tempted to do so myself if I'm not careful.

Suppose, for example, you've been spending the last few days ordering a new printer for your office. Your boss says to you, "How about sending me a memo and letting me know where things stand." You might be tempted to organize your memo by chronology—the way things happened:

First Try: Organizing by Chronology

On July 7, you asked me to order a new laser printer for our office. On that same day, I contacted Tom Milner on our computer liaison staff and began coordinating our request with him. Tom told me that we have the funds and the kind of printer we want is on the authorized list. Therefore, Tom gave us permission to make the buy.

On July 9, I called the printer company and found out the exact price ($3,799). Later that day, I contacted Susan in purchasing. Together, Susan and I filled out the request for the printer.

On July 11, Ms. Montgomery okayed the order and sent it to the printer company.

On July 14, I confirmed that the printer company received our order. The salesman I spoke with said we will have the printer tomorrow morning.

Takes forever to get to the bottom line, doesn't it? You can see, though, that the writer simply followed the chronology of what happened, tracking the purchase step by step for the boss.

You can see how easily a writer could be tempted into that chronological order. But what does the boss really want to know? Certainly not a blow-by-blow account of the process. Remember, the request was this: "Let me know where things stand." Keeping that in mind, let's try a different start—an opening statement:

Rewrite: Using an Opening Statement

We'll be getting our laser printer tomorrow. According to the salesman at the printer company, we can expect it at 9:30 tomorrow morning.

It will cost $3,799.

Approval was simple: Tom Milner (on our computer liaison staff) authorized it quickly. Susan Dobson (in purchasing) was very helpful preparing the order. Ms. Montgomery okayed the order and sent it out without incident.

Notice that the second memo gets to the point right away: the printer is coming tomorrow. Notice also that the memo is much shorter. That often happens. When you begin with an opening statement, you're much less likely to put in anything irrelevant. So the opening statement helps keep your reader on track—and *you* (the writer), too.

Should You Delay the Main Point for Bad News?

Rarely. Let's consider two kinds of "bad news":

- something bad that happened
- a recommendation your reader won't like

We'll start with something bad that happened. Let's say you're the boss and you lost a contract. Do you want that information buried near the end of a letter from your potential client?

Wouldn't you prefer to hear the "bad news" right away? You certainly don't want to slog through the detailed procedures the client used in choosing a contractor.

How about a recommendation your reader won't like? Subordinates often feel a boss will reject a recommendation quickly if it's up front, so they prefer to lead the boss step by step through their arguments. That way, the boss will reach the same conclusion they have reached. But facts and arguments are often hard to understand without context—without the bottom line, the recommendation. Therefore, the boss may only be confused if the main point is at the end—not impressed. Again, my recommendation is to start with your recommendation, no matter how controversial it is.

Be careful with your tone, though. For example, you probably wouldn't want to say this if your boss has been adamantly opposed: "We must hire a new manager as soon as possible."

But you could soften the tone and say something like this: "I know you don't think we should hire a new manager now, but I really think we need to. Please let me explain my reasons."

So you do need to treat bad news differently, but the difference is tone, not organization.

Should You State the Main Point with Facts and Figures?

Tom Murawski, a consultant and leader in the plain English movement, says, "Facts and figures speak for themselves—don't they?" He adds right away, "Of course not. *You* need to speak for them."

I agree. Too often as writers we're so involved with our data— our facts and figures—that they seem to point to obvious conclusions for us. But when we present facts and figures in a report, we use them to make a point. It's not very smart to leave out that point—the reason the facts and figures are there in the first place.

So tell the reader what the facts and figures mean—and do so *before* presenting them, not after. For example, don't do something like this:

First Try: Facts and Figures Alone

April 15, the order arrived at 9:15. Then on April 16, the order arrived at 9:35. On the next day, April 17, the order arrived at 8:55.

Huh? The facts and figures are supposed to be speaking for themselves, but they're not saying much, are they? Let's try again—this time adding a bottom line at the end (not the best place for it):

Second Try: Bottom Line Last

April 15, the order arrived at 9:15. Then on April 16, the order arrived at 9:35. On the next day, April 17, the order arrived at 8:55.

Therefore, we received the orders on time only one day: April 17. Orders are due at 9:00.

Better. The facts and figures are finally saying something, but now they're waiting too long to say it. So let's put the bottom line where it belongs—up front:

Third Try: Bottom Line First

We received the orders on time only one day: April 17. Orders are due at 9:00.

> Here's what happened:
>
> April 15, the order arrived at 9:15. Then on April 16, the order arrived at 9:35. On the next day, April 17, the order arrived at 8:55.

The memo still doesn't quite work, does it? The beginning is better, but the specific facts and figures don't have conclusions before them. Wouldn't it be better to explain whether *each order* was on time, rather than forcing the reader to take the time to compute the delay? After all, the very reason for those dates and times is to make a point about each one (whether the order was late or on time).

So for this version (the final one!), let's make those points:

Final Version: Conclusions Before Facts

We received the orders on time only one day: April 17. Orders are due at 9:00.

Here's what happened:

- *April 15.* The order was 15 minutes late (arriving at 9:15).
- *April 16.* The order was 35 minutes late (arriving at 9:35).
- *April 17.* The order was on time (arriving at 8:55).

The final version is longer, but it should save the reader time—and frustration, too.

The Opening Summary

The opening *statement* is a terrific way to begin a short document, but for a longer document, you probably want to say more than just a sentence or so. The way to do that is to use an opening *summary.*

An opening summary answers this question: "If I have only a few sentences—*total*—to tell my reader what's in this document, what would those sentences be?"

An Air Force general once told me his way of communicating the idea of an opening summary. He said to pretend you're getting on the elevator with your boss, and the boss asks for a quick summary of what's going on with your project. You need to finish by the time the elevator reaches the fourth floor. What would you say? The general called that an "elevator briefing."

So an opening summary is like an elevator briefing except:

- an opening summary is written
- an opening summary is just a beginning—the rest of the document immediately follows

Think of an opening summary as the first paragraph or so of a document—giving a complete overview of what follows. Like its relative, the opening *statement,* it doesn't say only what you're going to cover: it tells what you're actually going to conclude, recommend, or request.

Let's look at an example. Here's an opening summary from a two-page memo asking the boss for permission to buy an expensive laser printer and the software to get the most out of it:

An Opening Summary

SUBJECT: Proposal for a PostScript Laser Printer and Desktop Publishing

We need to improve the quality of the documents and proposals we're producing in our division.

To add a polished and professional look to our work, I

> recommend we buy a PostScript laser printer plus the software for our secretaries to do desktop publishing.
>
> The total cost would be about $6,500.

The rest of the memo then gives the details: why buy the laser printer, why buy the desktop publishing software, what the detailed costs are, and what the implementation plan is.

As the boss, wouldn't you appreciate the opening summary before all those facts and arguments?

So the main point of this chapter is simply to get to the point—with an opening statement for something short and with an opening summary for something longer.

Don't you wish everything in your "in" box started that way?

CHAPTER 4

Layout: Adding Visual Impact

When I give presentations on writing, my audiences usually consider layout to be the most important topic I cover.

What is layout, anyway? On its simplest level, it is whatever goes into the "look" of the page: something that appears open and inviting probably has good layout; something that appears cluttered and *un*inviting probably has bad layout.

The look of a page is important, but we'll see that good layout has two other terrific advantages:

- Good layout shows the reader—visually—your organization.
- It also helps you—the writer—be organized in the first place.

Layout is much more than packaging a document: it is the driving force behind organization. People who are aware of the techniques of good layout almost always write with good organization.

In this chapter, I'll cover three techniques for good layout:

- use short paragraphs
- use headings
- use bullets and other lists

These techniques are important at all times and *absolutely crucial* when the content of your writing is complex—as business

37

writing often is. Let's look at each of these techniques in more detail.

Use Short Paragraphs

Too often, the standard layout for business writing is wall-to-wall words. You've no doubt seen such pages. They look something like this (don't read—just look at the layout):

Do You Want To Read This?

This memo asks for your authorization to rent three computers for $900 total cost. We've ordered three personal computers to work on the Laredo project, but the supplier can't get them to us until June 1. Because we must start the project sooner, we need to rent other computers in the meantime. This memo gives you the details. I fully expect the new computers by June 1. The reason they are late is that the manufacturer is behind—demand has been much greater than anticipated. According to our supplier (Mr. Ted Ronson), we will not be able to get our three computers until June 1. To keep us as his customers, Mr. Ronson has added a penalty clause, guaranteeing the computers by then or else taking $1,000 off the price of each one. That sounds like a firm commitment to me, so I expect the computers by then. By the way, we have dealt extensively with Mr. Ronson during the past 3 years, and he has always been honest and reliable. Our delivery date for the Laredo project is September 20, so we cannot afford to wait until June (when the new computers arrive) to get started. We have found another dealer who will rent computers to us until June. These rental computers are not powerful enough to handle all the data we will ultimately generate on the project, but they will allow us to get started. We can then transfer the data to our new computers when they arrive in

---

June. Mr. Ronson will split the rental cost with us, so we pay
$900 and he pays $900. . . .

Not very appealing, is it? Now let's simply change the shape of
the words by arranging them into more appealing paragraphs:

Better Layout: With Short Paragraphs

This memo asks for your authorization to rent three computers for $900 total cost.

We've ordered three personal computers to work on the
Laredo project, but the supplier can't get them to us until
June 1. Because we must start the project sooner, we need
to rent other computers in the meantime. This memo gives
you the details.

I fully expect the new computers by June 1. The reason
they are late is that the manufacturer is behind—demand
has been much greater than anticipated. According to our
supplier (Mr. Ted Ronson), we will not be able to get our
three computers until June 1.

To keep us as his customers, Mr. Ronson has added a penalty clause, guaranteeing the computers by then or else taking $1,000 off the price of each one. That sounds like a
firm commitment to me, so I expect the computers by then.
By the way, we have dealt extensively with Mr. Ronson
during the past 3 years, and he has always been honest and
reliable.

Our delivery date for the Laredo project is September 20,
so we cannot afford to wait until June (when the new computers arrive) to get started. We have found another dealer
who will rent computers to us until June.

These rental computers are not powerful enough to handle
all the data we will ultimately generate on the project, but

> they will allow us to get started. We can then transfer the
> data to our new computers when they arrive in June.
>
> Mr. Ronson will split the rental cost with us, so we pay $900
> and he pays $900. . . .

Looks better, doesn't it? So far, I have these tips on paragraphs:

- Use short paragraphs.
- Always start with an especially short paragraph—nobody
  likes to begin reading anything that starts with a long paragraph. In fact, it's often a good idea to start with a short
  paragraph that contains your main point—as the example
  does.

A question often comes up about this time: "But isn't a paragraph a paragraph? Can we start paragraphs just anywhere?"

We can't start paragraphs anywhere, but there are many op-
tions. The old (un)truism is this: "Each paragraph should represent a separate thought. Some thoughts take longer than others;
therefore, some paragraphs may be very long."

To some extent, paragraphs do represent separate thoughts,
but what is a "thought," anyway? Every sentence contains at least
one thought and probably several. True, a new paragraph can
signal the next major thought, but business writing has a better
technique: headings. If you use headings—and I highly recommend them—you can paragraph almost visually beneath them.
The headings show the boundaries of the major "thoughts."

Also, think about newspapers—how long are their paragraphs? Their paragraphs are short because long paragraphs
would be quite forbidding in narrow newspaper columns.

In fact, if you give the same text to a newspaper editor and to
a textbook editor to divide into paragraphs, you'd get different
results: the newspaper editor would give you many short paragraphs; the textbook editor would give you slightly longer ones

(because textbook columns are much wider). In other words, both editors would paragraph—to some extent—visually.

And that's what I recommend you do, too. Now let's look at a related topic.

Use Headings

Just using short paragraphs isn't good enough. You also need to show your organization—visually—to your readers. A good way to do that is with headings. Think of headings as "labels" for the parts of your document.

For example, the memo we just worked with has short paragraphs, but it doesn't have labels for the various parts. Let's improve it one more step by adding those "labels":

Better Layout: With Headings

This memo asks for your authorization to rent three computers for $900 total cost.

We've ordered three personal computers to work on the Laredo project, but the supplier can't get them to us until June 1. Because we must start the project sooner, we need to rent other computers in the meantime. This memo gives you the details.

When Will the New Computers Arrive?

I fully expect the new computers by June 1. The reason they are late is that the manufacturer is behind—demand has been much greater than anticipated. According to our supplier (Mr. Ted Ronson), we will not be able to get our three computers until June 1.

To keep us as his customers, Mr. Ronson has added a penalty clause, guaranteeing the computers by then or else taking $1,000 off the price of each one. That sounds like a firm commitment to me, so I expect the computers by then. By the way, we have dealt extensively with Mr. Ronson during the past 3 years, and he has always been honest and reliable.

Why Do We Need To Rent Computers Temporarily?

Our delivery date for the Laredo project is September 20, so we cannot afford to wait until June (when the new computers arrive) to get started. We have found another dealer who will rent computers to us until June.

These rental computers are not powerful enough to handle all the data we will ultimately generate on the project, but they will allow us to get started. We can then transfer the data to our new computers when they arrive in June.

How Much Will Renting the Computers Cost?

Mr. Ronson will split the rental cost with us, so we pay $900 and he pays $900. . . .

Here are some quick tips on headings:

- Put more space above a heading than below it—so the heading visually belongs to the text it labels.
- Make the headings actually communicate with your readers (such as "When Will the New Computers Arrive?" instead of "Computer Arrival").
- Feel free to have more than one paragraph below a heading.

As you can see, headings are an important key to good business writing. They can also help you as a supervisor of writers. Suppose, for example, you're managing a large writing project. If you ask your people to use headings when they write, you know what you'll get? Not just headings, but organization, too. It's hard for people to use headings without being organized. Headings are the "little thing that does the big thing": a technique of layout that forces good organization. At the very least, headings require people to arrange their document into blocks of information instead of scattering ideas throughout. Headings also often keep people from using a chronological organization, which, because it usually buries the main point, often isn't appropriate.

Use Bullets and Other Indented Lists

Headings are terrific—and so are indented lists. As you can tell, I seldom write more than a page or so without using them somewhere. Just as headings show organization for the blocks of information in a document, lists often show organization within paragraphs.

A Quick Example: The Value of Lists

Business writing often has lists in it somewhere, and organized writers use lists particularly often. A list is all right as part of the text of a paragraph, but it's usually more effective if it's indented.

For example, read this sentence:

A List—But Not Indented

Three satellites are in geosynchronous orbit at 23,000 miles over the equator: Satellite I is at 55 degrees west longitude, Satellite II is at 70 degrees west longitude, and Satellite III is at 140 degrees west longitude.

Next, see how much better the layout is when we indent the list:

A List: Indented with Bullets

Three satellites are in geosynchronous orbit at 23,000 miles over the equator:

- Satellite I is at 55 degrees west longitude.
- Satellite II is at 70 degrees west longitude.
- Satellite III is at 140 degrees west longitude.

Indenting helps untangle that technical information.

A Second Example: Bullets or Numbers?

Here's another example—a set of instructions—that could benefit from indented lists. As you read this example, try to decide if it's organized or not:

Confusing Layout

To set up this laptop computer, you must first take the following steps. The dual latches mounted on the top of the computer must be pushed outward to release the top/monitor assembly, and then the top/monitor assembly must be moved to an oblique angle with the unit base. Disk Drive A must be released by pushing the release switch away from the operator. The operating system disk must then be inserted into Disk Drive A and the latch on Disk Drive A returned to its closed position. The I/O switch then must be manually placed into the "I" position by pushing it away from the operator, thereby placing the computer in the on position.

This paragraph doesn't seem organized, does it? But it *is*: it tells us, step by step, how to set up a laptop computer. The problem isn't poor *organization*; the problem is poor *layout*.

So let's take a first step to improve the layout by using bullets:

Better Layout: Bulleted List

To set up this laptop computer, you must take the following steps:

- Push the dual latches mounted on top of the computer outward to release the top/monitor assembly.
- Move the top/monitor assembly to an oblique angle with the unit base.
- Push the release switch on Disk Drive A away from you to release the drive.
- Insert the operating system disk into Disk Drive A.
- Close the latch on Disk Drive A.
- Push the I/O switch away from you to turn on the computer.

The paragraph now isolates each step visually. It also starts all listed items with verbs so the beginnings will be the same. That's called parallelism.

Even though the layout is much better for that paragraph (visually revealing the good organization that was already there), there's still a better way: a numbered list.

I suggest numbered lists when the order of the items is especially important; otherwise, use bulleted lists. In the paragraph we've been dealing with, the order of the items *is* especially important, showing the steps in the necessary order for setting up a laptop computer. So my final solution would be a numbered list, like this:

Even Better: A Numbered List

To set up this laptop computer, you must take the following steps:

1. Push the dual latches mounted on top of the computer outward to release the top/monitor assembly.
2. Move the top/monitor assembly to an oblique angle with the unit base.
3. Push the release switch on Disk Drive A away from you to release the drive.
4. Insert the operating system disk into Disk Drive A.
5. Close the latch on Disk Drive A.
6. Push the I/O switch away from you to turn on the computer.

Chapter 8, "More on Headings and Bullets," will give you further advice on spacing and punctuation for bulleted and numbered lists.

Do you see the advantage of good layout? It helps readers see a document's organization: the headings label the blocks of information; the indented lists isolate the facts, steps, arguments.

Even more important, good layout helps *produce* good organization. Writers who are aware of the techniques of good layout think about it *as* they write, not afterward. And as they write, they naturally form their ideas into blocks of information, and they isolate many of their facts, steps, and arguments into lists.

Thus, the techniques of good layout can actually be the driving force behind good organization.

CHAPTER 5

A Model for Writing:
Putting It All Together

This chapter presents a model you can use for much of your business writing—a "template" that will hold the ideas in many documents. These documents can be short (like memos) or long (like reports or even books).

If this sounds too good to be true, it isn't. I've used this model—or variations of it—many times, including for some of the most challenging and complex writing in government and business, writing involving complicated documents by auditors, lawyers, and accountants.

This model helps me when I write, and it can help you, too.

A Look at the Past

Before we look at the model, let's summarize what we've covered so far. I'll put the summary in the form of a checklist I often use:

A Checklist for Writers

Organization

1. Do you start with an opening statement or an opening summary?
2. Do you start each *section* of your document with the main point of that *section*?

47

Layout

1. Do you use short paragraphs (especially the first one)?
2. Do you use headings?
3. Do you use indented lists?

Style

1. Do you use the words you use when speaking?
2. Do you use a variety of punctuation?
3. Do you use personal pronouns?
4. Do you use contractions (sometimes)?

Of course you don't need to do all these things every time you write. But you should consider them almost every time. They'll work surprisingly often.

A Model for Writing

Now let's put everything together a different way—with a model for writing. This model is another way of visualizing the checklist I just showed you. But first, let's look at what the model *isn't*:

That's the typical model people use when they begin writing: the blank page. No wonder starting to write can be quite a chore!

So now let's examine the model I use frequently. Each box represents a block of information—perhaps only a paragraph or perhaps many paragraphs in a major section of a report:

A Model for Writing

Opening Statement or Opening Summary

Heading

Main Point
[Details]

Heading

Main Point
[Details]

Heading

Main Point
[Details]

And here's an explanation of the model:

1. Begin with an opening statement or an opening summary. An opening statement, you'll remember, is a sentence or so at the beginning that states your bottom line. An opening summary (used for longer documents) answers this question: "If I have only a few sentences—*total*—to tell my reader about this issue, what would those sentences be?"
2. Organize your content into blocks of related information. Those blocks don't have to be single paragraphs—they could be pages long (broken into short paragraphs, of course).
3. Label each of those blocks with a heading. Use subheadings, too, if the blocks are long.
4. Start each block by stating its main point. For example, if your heading is a question, begin the block by answering that question.
5. And use details—sometimes in bulleted or numbered lists—to support that main point.

Simple, isn't it?

The Model in Action

Let's apply the model. In Chapter 4, "Organization," we improved the layout of a memo step by step—first making shorter paragraphs and then adding headings.

That memo follows our model explicitly:

[Opening Summary]

This memo asks for your authorization to rent three computers for $900 total cost.

We've ordered three personal computers to work on the Laredo project, but the supplier can't get them to us until

June 1. Because we must start the project sooner, we need to rent other computers in the meantime. This memo gives you the details.

Heading: When Will the New Computers Arrive?

[Main Point First, Then Details]

I fully expect the new computers by June 1. The reason they are late is that the manufacturer is behind—demand has been much greater than anticipated. According to our supplier (Mr. Ted Ronson), we will not be able to get our three computers until June 1.

To keep us as his customers, Mr. Ronson has added a penalty clause, guaranteeing the computers by then or else taking $1,000 off the price of each one. That sounds like a firm commitment to me, so I expect the computers by then. By the way, we have dealt extensively with Mr. Ronson during the past 3 years, and he has always been honest and reliable.

Heading: Why Do We Need To Rent Computers Temporarily?

[Main Point First, Then Details]

Our delivery date for the Laredo project is September 20, so we cannot afford to wait until June (when the new computers arrive) to get started. We have found another dealer who will rent computers to us until June.

These rental computers are not powerful enough to handle all the data we will ultimately generate on the project, but they will allow us to get started. We can then transfer the data to our new computers when they arrive in June.

Heading: How Much Will Renting the Computers Cost?

[Main Point First, Then Details]

Mr. Ronson will split the rental cost with us, so we pay $900 and he pays $900. . . .

You can see this model can help untangle complex information for the reader—and for the writer. If you aim for this model when you begin writing, starting will be easier and you'll be more organized.

Does this model sound mechanical? Yes, it is. Too mechanical? I doubt it. The content of business writing can become extraordinarily complex; at the same time, readers are often busy. A mechanical organization is a blessing for a busy reader.

Think about yourself around April 15 each year. What kind of organization do you want for the instructions on filling out your income tax forms? If you're like me, you want the organization to be *absolutely clear—with no ambiguity whatsoever.*

Does the Model Work All the Time?

No—not all the time.

It works especially well for busy readers who want to get information as quickly as possible and then go on to something else. It works for people who *have* to read whatever you're writing and want the writing to be as painless as possible.

It doesn't work as well when you need to engage readers creatively and hold their attention with an entertaining style or innovative organization. Frankly, most people enjoy that kind of writing *off* the job but don't enjoy it *on* the job. They see the creative part as a waste of time (I don't, but I've found I'm in the minority).

Again, think of yourself as a reader: how much of the writing you read could benefit by following this model?

Does the Model Work for Technical Writing?

Yes, the model works *especially* well for technical, complex writing. In fact, the more complex the writing is, the more important this model is for the reader.

But just because the model works for complex writing doesn't mean it isn't suited for simple explanations and recommendations, too. The example in this chapter—about renting a computer—is relatively simple, and the model serves it well.

Do You Need To Follow All Parts
of the Model?

No, you don't need to follow all parts of the model all the time. For example, sometimes you might want to give the reader a little background before you can make your main point— whether for the entire document or part of it. You must still be careful, though, to keep the background to a minimum before you get to the point. Remember: readers know how to skip ahead.

When I have a lot of background to cover, I try to give the minimum up front, then state the main point, then add background if necessary. But a funny thing happens when I get the main point up front: I find I need much less background than I thought.

So keep the model in mind *before* and *as* you write. It's simple and effective.

POLISHING YOUR WRITING

CHAPTER 6

Punctuation

The first part of the book introduced you to the basics of plain English. Now let's add some polish. This chapter and the next two will polish your style, organization, and layout. The two chapters after that will help you avoid two "killers" of plain English—abstractness and passive voice.

We'll start with punctuation, a topic that has intimidated brave men and women for years. Yet it's not that hard—really. This section simplifies some rules and makes them easier to learn.

How often is punctuation important when you write? Every time. So take a few minutes now to greatly expand your arsenal. There's no need to spend the rest of your life restricted to only the period and the comma.

This chapter gives a few new ways to look at colons, dashes, and semicolons. Experiment with these marks and with those you already know how to use: parentheses, question marks, and underlining for emphasis. The results will be dramatic.

Why Is Punctuation Important?

Imagine, if you will, a string of words with no punctuation whatsoever:

Unpunctuated Words

xx xxxx xxx xxxxx xx x xxxxxxxxx xxxx xx x xxxxxxxx xx
xx xx x xxxx xxxxxx xxx xxxxxx xx xxxxxxxxxx xxx xxx
xxxxxx xxx xxxx xxxx xx xxxxxxxxxxx

There's a misconception that someone who is good at punctuating simply knows what punctuation should go where: a comma here, a semicolon there, a period at the end.

However, for someone who is good at punctuating, the words come out differently than for someone who is not. People who understand commas, semicolons, periods—and especially colons, dashes, and question marks—produce entirely different sentence structures from people who are not good at punctuation.

The result? Better sentences that have the emphasis—and ideas—in just the right places.

So don't think of punctuation as a way to go *wrong* (as a way to make mistakes). Instead, think of punctuation as a way to go *right*—as a way to say just what you mean in the best way possible.

Please note: This chapter gives you only a few of the most common and useful rules for colons, dashes, and semicolons. If you follow these rules, you will produce correct punctuation. But don't "correct" other people's writing just because they don't follow the rules here. There are other correct ways I don't include. (For a more complete look at punctuation, see any of the various handbooks on writing.)

The Colon

General Definition of the Colon

The colon is an extremely useful mark of punctuation. Think of it as an "arrow" that comes at the end of a complete sentence, pointing to some more useful information about what you just said. The colon can "point" to a word, to a list, to a sentence, even to a series of sentences or paragraphs.

Rules for the Colon

1. Use a colon (after a complete sentence) to point to a single word:
   - He started the business for one reason: money.
2. Use a colon (after a complete sentence) to point to a list:
   - He started the business for three reasons: adventure, fame, and money.
3. Use a colon (after a complete sentence) to point to another complete sentence:
   - He had always been a thrill-seeker: he once climbed the northwest face of Half Dome.
4. Use a colon (after a complete sentence) to point to a series of sentences or paragraphs:
   - He started the business for three reasons: He wanted adventure. He wanted fame. He wanted money.

Notice in each of these cases how the part after the colon receives emphasis. For instance, what's the difference between these two sentences?

- He started the business because he wanted money.
- He started the business for one reason: money.

Emphasis! The word *money* in the second sentence seems to have a spotlight on it.

Now—which is the better sentence? We can't say, can we? It depends on context and how much emphasis we want to give to *money*.

But who is the better writer: the one who can write both kinds of sentences or the one who can write only the one without the colon? Probably the one who writes both kinds is better because that person has more tools to control emphasis.

Now let's look at another important mark for plain English—the dash.

The Dash

General Definition of the Dash

Like the colon, the dash is an extremely useful mark of punctuation. It tells the reader that you are saying "something more" about what you just said—an example, an elaboration, a contradiction, whatever.

Handbooks once discouraged the dash as too informal for business writing; today we see the old books as too formal for plain English. Now the dash is a fully accredited mark of punctuation.

Rules for the Dash

1. Use a dash as you would a colon: as an "arrow" that comes at the end of a complete sentence, pointing to some more useful information about what you just said. Notice that the dash gives a slightly more informal feel to the sentence than a colon does:

   • He started the business for one reason—money.
   • He started the business for three reasons—adventure, fame, and money.
   • He had always been a thrill-seeker—he once climbed the northwest face of Half Dome.

   Normally you shouldn't use the dash to point to a series of sentences or paragraphs.

2. Use a pair of dashes (one on each side) to set off useful information in the middle of a sentence:

- He robbed the bank—the one just around the corner—for the sheer adventure.

The sentence is "He robbed the bank for the sheer adventure." The phrase "the one just around the corner" is in the middle of the sentence.

Question: What three marks could you put around that phrase?
Answer: a set of commas, a set of dashes, or a set of parentheses.

The difference? Dashes add emphasis to the phrase, commas give standard emphasis, and parentheses treat it like a whispered aside.

H. Ross Perot uses this rule very effectively in the article I quoted in Chapter 2:

- "We Americans have evolved from a tough, resilient people, willing to sacrifice for future generations, into a people who want to feel good now—at any price—and let the future take care of itself."

At any price—even though it's in the middle of a long sentence—stands out, doesn't it?

3. Use a dash (even where you might have no other punctuation) simply to emphasize the next idea:

- He robbed the bank—for adventure, notoriety, and greed.
- He robbed the bank for adventure, notoriety—and greed.

See how the dash puts emphasis on what follows? This is a common use of the dash in professional writing. H. Ross Perot uses this rule twice in his article:

- "It is hard to believe that the greatest nation in the world could be reduced to becoming a scrap salesman—but it's happening."
- "Put more directly, we have become credit junkies, shoot-

ing up huge sums of borrowed money on a government and personal level—looking for another high."

Again, you can see the effect the dash has on emphasis—like the hand gestures and vocal inflections we use when talking.

The Semicolon

General Definition of the Semicolon

The semicolon is slightly more formal than the colon and the dash. Professional writers today tend to use it much less than writers of several decades ago did.

Some people think of the semicolon as a "strong comma"—something between a comma and a period. That's true, but it's not the whole story.

The semicolon also has to separate equal grammatical units—an independent clause from another independent clause, or a dependent clause from another dependent clause, or a phrase from a phrase. The semicolon does not separate unequal units—like an *in*dependent clause from a *de*pendent clause.

In other words, think of the semicolon as a kind of "pivot": one idea is on *this* side of the semicolon; another idea is on *that* side of it. And on each side of the pivot point is a similar grammatical unit.

Rules for the Semicolon

1. Use a semicolon to join two (or more) complete sentences to show that those sentences are closely related.

   - In spring, the blossoms are beautiful on the apple trees; in autumn, the apples are a nuisance on the lawn.
   - The rock climber forgot to bring his rope and pitons; however, he remembered to bring the food.

Some people think a word like *however* always has a semicolon before it. No—the word *however* can move from the beginning of the independent clause to the middle or end of it. The semicolon still stays between the independent clauses—thus separating similar grammatical units:

- The rock climber forgot to bring his rope and pitons; he remembered, however, to bring the food.

2. Use a semicolon to separate items in series if any item in the series has commas in it.

Here's a sentence with incorrect punctuation—notice the confusion:

- *Confusing:* Many stars from the carnival were there: the ringmaster, Harpo and Groucho, the clowns, Feline, the lion tamer, Ursula, the bear, and, fortunately, Zorro, the bear tamer.

Now let's add semicolons—notice how much easier the sentence is to understand:

- *Correct:* Many stars from the carnival were there: the ringmaster; Harpo and Groucho, the clowns; Feline, the lion tamer; Ursula, the bear; and, fortunately, Zorro, the bear tamer.

A Final Word . . .

Try these marks—especially the dash and the colon, which are easy to use. And don't forget the question mark (which Chapter 2 covered) and other marks like underlining and parentheses. They all help substitute for the hand gestures and vocal inflection we use when talking.

CHAPTER 7

Executive Summaries
and Blueprints

This chapter adds some polish to the techniques on organization that the first part of the book covered.

You'll remember that most poor business writing has this organization:

Poor Organization

Fact
Fact
Fact
Logic
Logic
Therefore: Bottom Line

We've seen that organization many times—the writer taking us step by step to the logical conclusion. The problem is that without context, facts and logic can confuse us. The best way to add context is for the writer to start with the bottom line.

This organization usually works better:

Better Organization

Here's what I'm going to show you [the bottom line]. And here's how I reached that conclusion:
    fact
    fact
    fact
    logic
    logic

Isn't that the organization we prefer as readers? We want writers to get to the point and *then* tell us how they got there. If we're going from New York to Boston, we want to know at the beginning of the trip that Boston is our destination—not once we arrive.

This chapter adds two techniques of organization, two ways to help your readers gain an overview of what's to come:

- executive summaries
- blueprints

Let's look at these further.

Executive Summaries

Remember "opening summaries"? They answer this question: "If I have only a few sentences—*total*—to tell my reader what's in this document, what would those sentences be?" The opening summary begins a document, and the rest of the document immediately follows.

An executive summary is like an opening summary, with these differences:

- An executive summary is usually longer—sometimes a page (or even more).

- The *body* of the document doesn't immediately follow an executive summary; instead, the *beginning* of the document follows.

Essentially, an executive summary is for a longer document, and it is on a separate page, usually the first after the title page.

Who Reads an Executive Summary?

The answer seems obvious: executives, of course. That's true—but not the whole story.

The main reason for an executive summary *is* often to let a busy executive, usually a highly placed boss, read the summary instead of the document itself. If the executive summary is good, the executive can learn all the important bottom line information up front.

However, there are other important audiences:

- *Other people who are too busy to read the document.* The top boss may not be the only one who doesn't have time for the entire document but still needs the quick bottom line. Staff members, for example, may have such a need.
- *People wondering if they ought to read the document.* Without an executive summary, the only way to know if a document is relevant is to read it. But with an executive summary, the decision becomes much easier.
- *People who will read the entire document anyway.* Let's face it: *all* of us appreciate an executive summary. If we have to read the entire document anyway, the executive summary provides context—all the bottom-line information right there at the beginning.

An Example of an Executive Summary

Now let's look at an executive summary. This is the summary for a report to the head of a chain of shoe stores, urging a particular way for the stores to buy shoes.

An Executive Summary

Main Recommendation

This report recommends that we buy most of our shoes from wholesalers during actual visits to the wholesalers' warehouses.

The Problem

Now we buy shoes from the following sources:

- catalogs
- close-out lists
- phone contacts
- sales calls
- shows
- visits to wholesalers

The result? Too often we have shoes cluttering our store—shoes in strange colors, styles, and sizes that we have trouble selling. Worse, we often don't have the *right* colors, styles, and sizes to make sales.

What This Report Covers

In this report, I discuss the advantages and disadvantages of each way we buy shoes. And then I explain why the last way—visits to wholesalers—is better than each of the other ways.

The main advantage of visiting wholesalers? We can see the actual colors and styles we purchase, and we can check for quality and fit. Then we won't be stuck with shoes we can't sell.

You can see how valuable this summary would be to a reader preparing to read the lengthy report.

Cautions on Executive Summaries

Too often, writers forget the purpose of an executive summary —something to read *instead of* the entire report. As a result, two problems sometimes occur.

Sometimes the summary doesn't give the bottom line. The summary to the head of the shoe stores *does* give it: buy from wholesalers. However, what if the summary said only something like this?

Poor Executive Summary

This report recommends ways to buy our shoes. These are the sources the report considers:

- catalogs
- close-out lists
- phone contacts
- sales calls
- shows
- visits to wholesalers

The report examines each of these in detail and then makes a recommendation.

You can see that this version simply announces the topic; it doesn't give the recommendation (buy from wholesalers). Readers of executive summaries *especially* want the recommendation—that's often the main reason they're looking at the report.

A second problem with executive summaries is that they may use unfamiliar jargon. Often reports—especially technical ones—take care to define new terms before they use those terms later in the report. Poor executive summaries sometimes include those same terms—without defining them.

There's a great temptation to use the unfamiliar terminology in the summary because defining it might take up valuable space. That's true, but the answer is not to use the unfamiliar terminology anyway. The answer is to find plain English equivalents so you can talk in general terms.

For example, if I'm writing a report on types of writing needs for people in business, I wouldn't use the term *syntactic fluency* in the executive summary, even though that term might be crucial in the report itself. Instead, for the summary I'd use a plain English paraphrase: "help people learn to vary their sentence structure."

So think of executive summaries for longer documents. Your readers—almost all your readers—will find them invaluable.

Blueprints

A blueprint is simply a brief outline of what you'll cover. I had one near the beginning of this chapter:

A Sample Blueprint

This chapter adds two techniques of organization, two ways to help your readers gain an overview of what's to come:

- executive summaries
- blueprints

Let's look at these further.

For a building, a blueprint illustrates what the structure will look like; for a piece of writing, a blueprint tells the structure of what's to come.

Let's look at another blueprint, this from *Consumer Reports*, telling us how to buy a new car:

From *Consumer Reports*

Before you think of shopping for a car, do your homework. Approach your car-shopping methodically, in the following sequence:

- Narrow your choices of cars and equipment.
- Find out what the dealer paid the factory for the car.
- Shop more than one dealer.
- Keep the transaction as simple and straightforward as possible.

Let's examine each step in detail.

A blueprint works well with opening statements, opening summaries, and executive summaries. Those three techniques announce the bottom line. The blueprint then announces the organization of the document. Both pieces help readers understand what they're about to read.

Here are some tips for writing good blueprints:

- Use highlighting (such as bullets or numbers) to emphasize the blueprint list.
- Put a sentence after the blueprint telling your readers you're going to say more about it ("Let's examine each step in detail."). A bulleted or numbered list isn't necessarily a blueprint—it might be just a list, and the writer might change the topic immediately afterward. A sentence after the blueprint leaves no doubt for the reader.
- Use headings in the body of your document that match the key words in your blueprint. For example, the first heading in the *Consumer Reports* article on buying a car is "Narrow

Your Choices." The heading helps reinforce the structure of the document.

As I mentioned in Chapter 5, this may all seem mechanical. But when we're reading complex information, a clear organization is a huge benefit. Putting the main point up front and adding a blueprint are two easy ways for you to make your organization clear.

CHAPTER 8

More on Headings and Bullets

In Chapter 4, we looked at layout as an important way to show your document's organization. This chapter helps you add some polish to two techniques you learned there: headings and bullets.

By the way, there are no universal standards on how to use headings and bullets. We can go to a dictionary to find out how to spell *minuscule* and *pavilion*, but there's no "book" telling us how to handle layout. There may be rules *within* a company, but a different company will usually have different rules, if any at all.

So what I'm about to show you is the system I've developed over the years. It's not right or wrong. It's simply one system.

I'm especially indebted to Dr. Ginny Redish, famous for her work in plain English. Some key ideas in this chapter originated with her.

More About Headings

Just having headings isn't good enough. You want to use them well so they clearly indicate what's subordinate and what isn't. This section shows you how.

Using Our Educated Intuition

We all have an intuition, and exposure over the years to thousands of pages of writing has helped educate it on what headings work and what headings don't.

Suppose your document has this typical organization:

Organization of a Document

Major section of the document

   Subsection of the document

   Subsection of the document

Major section of the document

   Subsection of the document

   Subsection of the document

You'd want your headings to show—by the design of the headings—which is a major section of the document and which is a subsection.

These headings would *not* do that, would they:

Headings That Don't Work

This Is a Major Heading
xx xxx xxx xxxxxx xx xxx xx xxxx x xxxxxxx xxxxx xxxxx
xxxxxx xxxxxx xxxx xxx xxx xx xxxxxxxx xx xxx xxxxxx

XXXX XXXXXXXX XXXXXX XXX XXXX XXXXXX X XXXXXX XXXXX
XXXXX XXX

THIS IS A SUBHEADING

XX XXXXX XXX XXXXX XX X XXXXXX XXXX XX XXXX XXXXXXXX
XXXXXXXX XXX XXXXXX X XXXXXXXX XXXXXX XXXXX XXXXX
XXXXXX XXXXXXXXXX XXXXXXXX XXXXXXXX XXXX

THIS IS A SUBHEADING

XXX XXXX XXXXXX XXXX XX XXXXX X XXXXXXX XXX XXXX XXXX-
XX XXXX X X XXXXXX XXXXXXXXXXX XX XX XXXXX XX XXXXXX
XXX XXXXXXX XXXX XXXXXX XX XXXX XXXX XXXXXX

Our educated intuition says not: we expect all uppercase letters to be more important than mixed upper and lowercase letters.

Let's see what happens when we reverse those heading styles:

Headings That Do Work

THIS IS A MAJOR HEADING

XXX XXX XXXXXXXX XXXX XXXX XXXXX XXXX XX XXXXX XXXXX
XXXX XXXXXXX XXXXXX XXXXXX XX XX XXXXXXX XXXXX XXXXX
XX XXX XXXXX XX XXXXX XX XX XX XX

This Is a Subheading

XXX XXX XXX XXXX XX XX XXXXXX XX XXXXX XXXXX XX XXXX
XXX XX XXXXX XXXX XX XX XXXXXXXX XXXXX XXXXX XXXXX X
XXXX XX XXX XXXXXX X XXX XXXX XXX

This Is a Subheading

xxx xxx xxx xxxx xx xx xxxxxx xx xxxxx xxxxx xx xxxx
xxxxx xxxxx xxx xxxxx xxx xx xxxxx xxxx xx xx xxxxxxxxxx xx xxx xxxxxx x xxx xxxx xxx

Now our educated intuition agrees, doesn't it?

A System of Headings

Here's a system of headings that works with our educated intuitions. This system requires only the technology available on typewriters and simple printers—the ability to underline and use upper and lowercase:

Four Styles of Headings

CENTERED

xxxx xxxxxxx xxxxxx xxxxxx xx xx xxxxxxx xxxxx xxxxx
xx xxx xxxxx xx xxxxx xx xx xx xx

FLUSH LEFT—UPPERCASE ONLY

xxx xx xx xxxxx xxxxx xxx xxxx xx xx xx x x xxxx xxxxx
xxx xxxxxxx

Flush Left—Upper and Lowercase

xxxxx xxx xx xxxxx xxxxxx xxxxx xxxx xxxx xxxxxx xxxxxx xx xx xxxxx xxxxx xxx xxxx xx xx xx x x xxxx xxxxx
xxx xxxxxxx

<u>**Flush Left—Followed by Text**</u>. xxxx xxxx xx xxxxx xxxxx
xxx xxx xxx xxxx xx xx xxxxxx xx xxxxx

With this system, you can have four levels of headings.

Which two styles should you use if you have only two levels of subordination? I wouldn't use the first and second styles—they look too much alike. Instead, I'd use the *first* and *third* styles, like this:

Using Only Two Headings

THIS IS A MAJOR HEADING

xxxxx xxx xx xxxxx xxxxxx xxxxx xxxx xxxx xxxxxx xxxxxx xx xx xxxxx xxxxx xxx xxxx xx xx xx x x xxxx xxxxx
xxx xxxxxxx

This Is a Subheading

xxxxx xxx xx xxxxx xxxxxx xxxxx xxxx xxxx xxxxxx xxxxxx xx xx xxxxx xxxxx xxx xxxx xx xx xx x x xxxx xxxxx
xxx xxxxxxx

This is a Subheading

xxxxx xxx xx xxxxx xxxxxx xxxxx xxxx xxxx xxxxxx xxxxxx xx xx xxxxx xxxxx xxx xxxx xx xx xx x x xxxx xxxxx
xxx xxxxxxx

By using such different styles, you're less likely to confuse your readers.

What if you need only one level of heading? Then any style will do. I normally choose the third style, however, which is flush left—upper and lowercase. The reasons probably "split hairs":

- Upper and lowercase text is slightly easier to read.
- Reader's eyes return naturally to the left margin. Therefore, readers are slightly more likely to read a heading on the left-hand side.

Are There Other Ways To Make Headings?

There are many, many other ways of creating headings. With most computer printers, you can use bold typeface, different type sizes (larger for major headings), and different type families (Times or Helvetica, for instance). There's color, there's . . . but you get the idea. Remember, though: too many styles of headings in the same document can make it look cluttered and confusing. Today's technology has dangers as well as opportunities.

The important thing is for you to be aware that the style of heading is one consideration for anything you write. Once you've decided what kinds of headings you prefer, your choices can then be almost automatic for all writing you do afterward.

More About Bullets

As you can tell, I consider the bullet a magical device, a wonderful way to help untangle ideas and show readers the organization within paragraphs.

In Chapter 4, we looked at bulleted *lists*. This section looks at bulleted *paragraphs* and then discusses ways to add polish to the way you present both bulleted lists and bulleted paragraphs.

Let's start with the bulleted paragraph.

What Is a Bulleted Paragraph?

You needn't feel that bullets show only single words, phrases, or sentences, like this:

Bulleted List

After 3 months of examining your records for the past year, we have found the following:

- Your marketing division is systematically hiding its losses each month—totalling $300,000 for the past 6 months alone.

- The division manager and his assistant appear to be the only people involved.
- There were no other major discrepancies.

You can also have entire paragraphs—I think of them as *sub*-paragraphs—as bullets.

Bulleted Paragraphs

After 3 months of examining your records for the past year, we have found the following:

- Your marketing division is systematically hiding its losses each month—totalling $300,000 for the past 6 months alone. This may have been taking place for years—we did not have access to your records before last June.
- The division manager and his assistant appear to be the only people involved now. Some former employees may have been involved, however. For example, the former budget clerk just bought a Mercedes sports car and has moved to Hawaii. Perhaps he was involved, too.

Why use bulleted paragraphs? The usual answer: they show your reader the organization of your document. Normal paragraphing doesn't do that:

Normal Paragraphs

After 3 months of examining your records for the past year, we have found the following:

Your marketing division is systematically hiding its losses each month—totalling $300,000 for the past 6 months alone. This may have been taking place for years—we did not have access to your records before last June.

The division manager and his assistant appear to be the only people involved now. Some former employees may have been involved, however. For example, the former budget clerk just bought a Mercedes sports car and has moved to Hawaii. Perhaps he was involved, too.

All three of those paragraphs look the same, as though they're at the same level of subordination. Actually, as we've seen, the second and third paragraphs are subordinate to the first. Bulleted paragraphs show that relationship better.

For simple narrative, bulleted paragraphs would probably be overkill. But for explaining complex information, they make the reader's task just a little easier. I am particularly careful to use bulleted paragraphs when I'm presenting technical, legal, or financial information.

What Symbol Should You Use for Bullets?

There isn't just one symbol for bullets, so you don't have to have a printer with special fonts to write with them. Here are some perfectly acceptable ways for making the bullet symbol:

Ways To Make the Bullet Symbol

o Use a lowercase letter o. Fill it in with a black pen if you want to be fancy, but there's usually no need. The lowercase o by itself is a common way to make the bullet symbol.

> \- Use a single hyphen.
>
> * Use an asterisk.

These ways all work fine. (But you wouldn't want to use all three in the same list, as I've done here.)

By the way, if you check newspapers and magazines, you can find many different bullet symbols: small boxes, squiggles, check marks, graphic art (drawings of small pencils, for example), and so forth.

What Spacing Should You Use for Bulleted Lists and Paragraphs?

The reason for using bulleted lists and paragraphs is to isolate information, so you want to use plenty of white space. Here's a bulleted list that does just about everything wrong:

Poor Spacing

After 3 months of examining your records for the past year, we have found the following:
•Your marketing division is systematically hiding its losses each month—totalling $300,000 for the past 6 months alone.
•The division manager and his assistant appear be the only people involved.
•There were no other major discrepancies.

Not effective, is it? I suggest using this spacing instead:

Bulleted List

After three months of examining your records for the past year, we have found the following:

- Your marketing division is systematically hiding its losses each month—totalling $300,000 for the past six months alone.
- The division manager and his assistant appear to be the only people involved.
- There were no other major discrepancies.

The attached report discusses these three findings.

This spacing will help you "show off" your list so it can gain the attention it deserves. You can use this spacing for a numbered list, too. By the way, I'd doublespace between bulleted items for documents that aren't typeset.

How Should You Punctuate Bulleted Lists?

When you're using bulleted *paragraphs*, you don't have to worry about special punctuation—just punctuate normally. But when you're using bulleted *lists*, you may wonder whether to start with a capital letter and whether to put a period at the end. After all, some lists are only words or phrases.

There are two common methods: the traditional method and the contemporary method (which I use). The traditional method— still quite popular—simply keeps the punctuation the list would have if it were part of a normal paragraph. Here's a list that's part of a normal paragraph—it's not bulleted yet:

List in a Normal Paragraph

The order was late on April 15, late on April 16, and on time on April 17.

The traditional method would keep that same punctuation, pretending the list is still part of a regular sentence:

Traditional Method

The order was:

- late on April 15,
- late on April 16,
- and on time on April 17.

The contemporary method—gaining popularity—stops the pretense that there's a sentence and gets rid of the commas, the period, and the word *and*:

Contemporary Method

The order was:

- late on April 15
- late on April 16
- on time on April 17

Where's the period to end the sentence? I don't know. There simply isn't one. But readers are more likely to notice a period *there* than a period *missing*. The contemporary method places more importance on each item in the list having the same appearance than on pretending the list is still a "sentence."

So here's how the contemporary method handles punctuation and capitalization:

- If the listed item *is* a sentence, make it look like one (that is, start with a capital letter and put a period at the end).
- If the listed item *is not* a sentence, don't. That is, don't start with a capital letter and don't put any punctuation at the end.

Dr. Redish devised this method to cope with the many lists in computer manuals.

Let's look at several examples. You've seen the next one before. Notice that the items in it are *not* sentences, so they don't begin with capital letters or end with periods:

Items Are *Not* Sentences

The order was:

- late on April 15
- late on April 16
- on time on April 17

Now let's rewrite that example to make the items sentences. Notice that they now look like sentences—with capital letters and periods:

Items *Are* Sentences

Here's what happened to the orders:

- They were late on April 15.
- They were late on April 16.
- They were on time on April 17.

By the way, lists should never have some items that are full sentences and some that aren't. That violates parallelism. In other words, once you set up a pattern for a list, you must stick to it—*all* full sentences or *all* only phrases.

Sometimes, though, you have items that are only phrases but then you want to add a comment or two. What do you do? Do you start with a phrase and then add a sentence just after it? That wouldn't work. Well, here's a good solution involving a little rewriting (we saw this sample in Chapter 3):

Bulleted List with Headings

Here's what happened:

- <u>April 15</u>. The order was 15 minutes late (arriving at 9:15).
- <u>April 16</u>. The order was 35 minutes late (arriving at 9:35).
- <u>April 17</u>. The order was on time (arriving at 8:55).

This combines both chapter topics—bullets *and* headings. They work well separately; they work well together. And both make the reader's job much easier.

CHAPTER 9

Abstractness and Concreteness

So far this book has emphasized what to do. But this chapter and the next (on passive voice) tell you what *not* to do. In fact, no matter how well you do everything else, your writing will still be burdensome to your readers unless you avoid abstractness and passive voice. They're that bad—killers, in fact, of plain English.

This chapter will help you conquer one of those killers: abstractness. Let's begin by defining it.

What Is Abstract Writing?

Abstract writing is so general that readers constantly have to guess what it means. If I stopped there, that sentence would be abstract—you'd have to guess what *I* mean. So let's consider an example. Here's an abstract sentence by a university president describing his job:

Abstract

I solve long-term questions, and I solve short-term questions.

The sentence is in plain English, but it's not really memorable. By memorable, I don't mean deathless prose such as "Give me liberty or give me death!" I simply mean something we can remember by the time we finish the page. Abstract sentences don't pass the "memorable" test.

Now let's look at concrete writing—the actual version by that university president. Notice how much more effective it is:

More Concrete

I solve long-term questions like "What should the university be like in 10 years?" and "How can we get a curriculum more relevant to our students?"

I also solve short-term questions like "How can we get a new building for our administration?"

The concrete version gives us a better feel for the university president's job, doesn't it?

Abstract writing, then, is so vague that it asks us to stop reading and guess what it means. Normally we don't do that. Instead, we just keep reading, hoping for something better in the next sentence or the next paragraph. If there isn't anything better, we might just go to lunch.

Even if we make educated guesses to figure out the abstract writing, we can't be sure we've gotten the author's intended meaning. That's why professional writers take the guesswork out by supplying the missing information.

How Can You Be More Concrete?

Concreteness is crucial to good writing. The rest of the chapter looks at these three ways to be more concrete:

- Use "such as" statements.
- Tell brief stories.
- Make comparisons.

Use "Such As" Statements

A "such as" statement is a quick example (normally fairly short—from a word to a couple sentences). Let's look at some writing without "such as" statements. This is from a federal agency:

Abstract

AIDS involves difficult legal issues.

That statement is certainly true, but it won't have much impact. It probably won't find any brain cells to lodge in. Let's try again, this time adding two "such as" statements:

More Concrete

AIDS involves difficult legal issues. For example:

- Can we require members of our agency to take the AIDS test?
- If so, how much information about the results are we obligated to release to the public?

These "such as" statements help make the writing more memorable, don't they?

You can see that "such as" statements don't actually have to use the specific words "such as." They're just quick examples. One common place for these quick examples is in lists. Some lists, of course, don't need them:

A Concrete List

- carrots
- peas
- potatoes

Not exciting—but not abstract, either. In poor business writing, however, lists often are abstract. Let me show you an abstract list that auditors might run across in a regulation telling them how to write a report.

Auditors try to find out whether things are going well within an organization. If they find something wrong, that something is a "finding." This list tells auditors what a report of a finding should cover:

An Abstract List

These are the five elements of a finding you must cover in your report:

1. condition
2. cause
3. criteria
4. effect
5. recommendation

Abstract. Now for the concrete. Let's put in a quick explanation and then a "such as" statement after each of the five elements:

A More Concrete List

These are the five elements of a finding you must cover in your report:

1. *Condition.* What was the problem you found? Example: The nurses do not record the medicine they give their patients.
2. *Cause.* Why is the problem happening? Example: The nursing staff is 42% short of people, leaving no time for nurses to both give the medicine and record that they've given it.
3. *Criteria.* What requires the action in question? Example: Hospital Regulation 213.4 requires whoever gives medicine to record that fact.
4. *Effect.* What's the result of the action? Example: Patients could die or have worsened conditions if they receive too much or too little medicine.
5. *Recommendation.* What should the organization do to correct the situation? Example: Counsel all nurses and require supervisors to monitor the records.

You certainly noticed that the concrete version is much longer. That's true. But longer is not necessarily worse. The real issue is, "Which version communicates more efficiently to the reader?" Sometimes more writing is better than less. If you're an auditor reading that regulation, which version is more likely to result in a good audit report?

You may wonder when you should use "such as" statements. The answer: whenever your reader won't understand the abstract version alone. Professional writers use them frequently.

In fact, a good suggestion for supervisors is to tell your people to use lots of these two transitions (or words like them): *for instance* and *for example.* The result will almost always be more concreteness.

Tell Brief Stories

We all love stories. What's our reaction when a speaker says, "Let me tell you what happened last Saturday evening"? Our ears perk up, and we suddenly pay attention.

The same thing happens to readers—a story perks them up. But more important, a story can be an excellent way to communicate something abstract. Notice how a brief story can help define the abstract term *capital gain*:

A Story About Jeannette

Jeannette graduated from college a year ago and decided she should invest some of her savings in the stock market. After asking her friends, she decided to buy 20 shares of CD Player, Inc. Each share cost Jeannette $12, so her total cost was $240.

If Jeannette sells that stock next year for more than $12 a share, she will have a capital gain. For example, if she sells all 20 shares for $15, she will have a capital gain of $3 a share—or $60 total.

If she sells her stock for less than $12, she will have a capital loss.

See how the story helps make something abstract—like capital gain—easier to understand? In this case, it doesn't tell the whole story, but it's certainly a good beginning.

Another way to tell a story is to use the reader as a character. In other words, *Jeannette* becomes the word *you*:

A Story About *You*

You graduated from college a year ago and decide to invest some of your savings in the stock market. After asking your friends, you buy 20 shares of CD Player, Inc. Each share costs you $12, so your total cost is $240.

If you sell that stock next year for more than $12 a share, you will have a capital gain. For example, if you sell all 20 shares for $15, you will have a capital gain of $3 a share— or $60 total.

If you sell your stock for less than $12, you will have a capital loss.

Casting *you* as character in the story makes the situation more immediate to the reader.

Either way works well. The guides we find in bookstores on how to pay our income taxes use this technique often—telling stories to make abstract concepts clear to us.

Make Comparisons

If there's one technique of concreteness that separates amateurs from professionals, it's that professionals tend to use many comparisons. However, comparisons have a plus and a minus:

- *The plus.* A good comparison will probably be the most memorable part of a piece of writing.
- *The minus.* A good comparison is hard to think of.

Nevertheless, many people have thought of excellent ones. John D. MacDonald, a famous novelist, used comparisons often in his writing. Here's one telling us about news stories:

From *The Dreadful Lemon Sky*

But a news story is a fragile thing. It is like a hot air balloon. It needs a constant additive of more hot air in the form of new revelations, new actions, new suspicions. Without this

> the air cools, the big bag wrinkles, sighs, settles to the ground, and disappears.

We know that comparisons appear in novels, but do they appear in business writing? Yes. Here's an extended comparison urging us to pay millions of dollars for expensive weather radars:

Comparison: Weather Radars

The United States has used weather radars since the 1950s—which is precisely why we need replacements: the current system is dated and becoming increasingly hard to fix when it breaks.

For a comparison, imagine you are still using the black and white television set your family bought in the 1950s. The set would be technically outdated:

- It receives black and white pictures and monophonic sound even though color and stereo are now available.
- It uses vacuum tube technology—and replacement tubes are expensive (if you can find them).

With a television set almost 40 years old, you'd be thinking about replacing it. Well, many weather radars are about 40 years old, too. And that's why we need NEXRAD—the *NEX*t Generation *RAD*ar—for our weather forecasters.

We're probably not convinced on the spot, but the comparison does help make the point. Certainly we can't imagine watching a 40-year-old television when something far better is available.

So check your writing for abstractness. Are there places you could add "such as" statements? Brief stories? Comparisons? Your writing may grow longer, but it will probably communicate much better.

CHAPTER 10

Passive Voice

If you've heard one outcry against bad business and government writing, it's "Too much passive voice!" That's a good outcry, because bureaucratic writers significantly overuse it. Passive voice isn't always bad, but lots of it absolutely kills readability.

Passive voice is an extremely important concept—the small investment you make in learning about it will repay you time and again, probably beginning with the next business document you write.

By the way, the advice to "write the way you talk" applies in full force here: we seldom talk in passive voice, yet many people consistently write in it. If you really try to write the way you talk, you will almost certainly write in active voice.

So by knowing about active and passive voice, you can check yourself to be sure your writing is like your talking.

What Are Active and Passive Voice?

Does this sound bureaucratic?

Passage 1

The requested work papers will be provided. However, recommendations cannot be given until further discussions have been held with our subcontractors.

It's in passive voice. Now let's put it in active voice:

Passage 2

We will provide you the work papers you requested. However, we cannot give you our recommendations until we hold further discussions with our subcontractors.

See the difference? The first passage is in *passive voice*, typical of the bureaucratic style of writing. The second passage is in *active voice*, a key characteristic of plain English.

Now *especially* notice the next two paragraphs—they're the most important ones in the chapter. If you follow them, you'll understand what passive voice is.

In Passage 1. What's the subject of the first sentence? *Work papers.* What's the verb? *Provided.* Are the work papers doing the providing? No. Therefore, the subject is passive—it's not doing anything. It's being done to. Since the subject is acted upon, the verb is in passive voice.

In Passage 2. What's the subject of the first sentence? *We.* What's the verb? *Provide.* Is the subject (*We*) doing the providing? Yes. Therefore, the subject is active. It's doing something. Since the subject is the actor in the sentence, the verb is in active voice.
  Simply, then:

- When the *subject is acted upon*, the verb is in passive voice.
- When the *subject is the actor*, the verb is in active voice.

That makes sense, doesn't it?

How Can You Identify Active and Passive Voice?

One way to identify passive voice is to check each subject to see if it's the "actor" or the "acted upon." That can be time consuming.

Luckily, there's a more objective way to check. Passive voice has all three of these characteristics:

Three Characteristics of Passive Voice

1. a form of the verb *to be* (*is, am, are, was, were, be, been,* or *being*)

   AND

2. a past participle (a verb ending in *-ed* or *-en* except irregular verbs like *kept*)

   AND

3. a prepositional phrase beginning with *by*

Let's look at another passive sentence:

Passive Voice

The trailer *was* pull*ed by* the car.

Notice that our passive sentence does, indeed, have all three characteristics:

- a form of the verb *to be*: *was.*
- a past participle: *pulled.*
- a prepositional phrase beginning with *by*: *by the car.*

These passive sentences have all three characteristics, too:

- The door *is* being clos*ed by* the conductor.
- The copier has *been* turn*ed* on *by* Susan.
- The result will *be* post*ed by* personnel.

Wouldn't life be simple if that were the end of it? But, alas, there is one important exception to these three characteristics: sometimes there is no prepositional phrase beginning with the word *by*. For example, all of these sentences are still passive:

- The door is being closed.
- The copier has been turned on.
- The result will be posted.

The first sentence we worked with in this chapter also is missing the *by* prepositional phrase:

- The requested work papers will be provided.

But there could be a *by* prepositional phrase—you could add one easily (if you knew the information) without changing the structure of the rest of the sentence. So it's still a good characteristic. It's also extremely important, as you'll see later in this chapter.

What's the Difference: Voice and Tense?

Some people confuse passive voice and past tense. That's like confusing *big* and *green*—two adjectives that describe completely different characteristics of something.

Voice, as we've seen, refers to whether or not the subject is the actor in the sentence. *Tense*, on the other hand, simply refers to the time an action takes place (past, present, future).

Here's a verb with passive voice:

Passive Voice and Past Tense

The file cabinet was moved.

So it's passive voice, but what tense is it? As you can see—past tense. Here's the same sentence—still passive voice—in *present* tense:

Passive Voice and Present Tense

The file cabinet is being moved.

We can also have the same idea in *active voice*, past or present tense.

So don't confuse voice and tense. And if you hear people confusing the two, you know they don't really understand passive voice. Or past tense, either.

What's the Matter with Passive Voice?

The problem isn't simply passive voice. The problem is that amateur writers use it about five times as often as professional writers do, and that's a conservative estimate for typical government and business writing.

Remember earlier I said one way to identify passive voice is that there's a prepositional phrase beginning with the word *by*?

With a *By* Phrase

The door is being closed *by the conductor.*

And I also said that you can sometimes eliminate that phrase and still have a perfectly grammatical passive sentence?

Without a *By* Phrase

The door is being closed.

The problem is that the object of the preposition in the *by* prepositional phrase is not just any word: *it's the actor—the one doing whatever the verb says.* Often, it's crucial information. Consider, once again, the first sample of passive voice in this chapter:

Passage 1

The requested work papers *will be provided.* However, recommendations *cannot be given* until further discussions *have been held* with our subcontractors.

All the verbs are passive, and there are no *by* prepositional phrases. That means there are no *actors*—the ones doing whatever the verb says!

No wonder it's hard to read! The "actors" were perfectly obvious to the writer, who knew the idea she wanted to communicate. But the readers—you and I—don't know, but need to. So one of the biggest problems with passive voice is that it often leaves out crucial information: who did it.

There's a second problem. Even if the *by* prepositional phrase is there, the actor comes at the end of the sentence.

Since the key information in passive voice appears at the end of the sentence (if at all), we've often lost track of the first part of the sentence by the time we get to the end—particularly in complex bureaucratic writing. Then we have to reread. Or say "Forget it!" and read further without understanding the passive sentence.

And what if the next sentence is passive? And the one after that? In fact, we end up skipping a lot of sentences.

Why Do People Write Passive Voice?

One reason people write passive voice is to *intentionally* leave out the actor. For example, timid bosses wouldn't want to write this sentence:

Would You Say This?

I have decided everybody must work this weekend.

The actor is *I*—who may seem pretty exposed to gripes and other criticism from the people who can't go sailing or skiing during the weekend. So some bureaucrats, to avoid responsibility, tend to put such a sentence in passive voice and then eliminate the *by* prepositional phrase:

Passive Magic

It has been determined ~~BY ME~~ that you must work this weekend.

Now, through the magic of passive voice, the boss is in the clear. After all, who can find the subject of that sentence—*It*—to gripe to?

But this reason—avoiding responsibility—actually accounts for only a small percentage of the sentences in passive voice.

After all, only a few key sentences in any document are ones in which people must accept or avoid responsibility.

Here's a second reason people write passively: they try to avoid using personal pronouns like *we* and *you*. Unfortunately, unless they use personal pronouns, passive voice is the natural result.

So pronouns are the key. In fact, bosses who say, "Write in plain English, but don't use any personal pronouns" are like home builders who say, "Build me a nice house, but—hey—I don't like hammers, so don't use them." Hard to build a house, and hard to write plain English, too.

And a third reason people write passively? They just do. They start in passive voice and then just stay there. Without much effort at all, they could easily have written the same ideas actively.

Is Passive Voice Ever All Right?

Of course. Three times:

- when you don't know the actor ("John was murdered.")
- when the actor is unimportant to the point you're making ("The Congressman was re-elected.")
- when the emphasis is clearly not on the actor but on the acted upon ("What happened to the little girl? *The little girl was rescued.*")

So don't think of passive voice as always bad. Think of it as putting unnecessary strain on the reader. Use passive when you need to—but be careful of overusing it. Seldom (if ever) have readers suffered because the writer overused *active voice*.

A Final Word

Is writing active voice worth the effort? Yes! It can make a dramatic impact on the readability of your writing. In fact, if you habitually write passive voice, I can almost guarantee that your readers have been skimming in frustration and confusion. That's not what you want your readers to do, is it?

Well . . . some of the time, perhaps. But recognizing active and passive voice will help you decide when.

Do you want to find out if you're writing passive voice? Take some of your recent business writing and circle all the passive verbs on one full page. If you find only two or three, you're doing fine. If, on the other hand, you find many more. . . .

FINAL WORDS

CHAPTER 11

The Writing Process: Computers and More

So far this book has been totally concerned with the *product* of your writing: your document should start with the bottom line, use good layout, have a clear style, and avoid abstractness and passive voice. This chapter and the next are about the *process* of writing:

- How can you get words on paper easily?
- How, as a supervisor, can you get the best writing from your people?

This chapter discusses getting words on paper easily. Here's what it covers:

- What's a good writing process?
- What's the role of the computer in the writing process?
- What are some general tips on writing?

Let's get started.

What's a Good Writing Process?

Is this the writing process you learned?

Typical Writing Process—Old View

Prewriting

1. Think hard.
2. Write an outline.

Writing

1. Follow your outline.
2. Write quickly without worrying about revisions.

Rewriting

1. Make sure you followed your outline.
2. Fix any errors.

Well, there's surely some truth there, but there are some half-truths, too.

The Role of the Outline

What's the role of an outline? Should you have one? Most business people I speak with confess: they rarely use an outline, and they virtually never use a formal outline (you know—I, A, B, II, A, B).

Outlines do have advantages, though. It's always helpful to know where you're going before you start. But sometimes writers simply aren't quite sure where they're going *until* they write; that is, as they struggle to put thoughts into those elusive things called words, learning takes place: new ideas emerge and old ideas take new shape. We've all had that experience.

In other words, sometimes we have trouble writing an effective outline at the beginning of the writing process. Starting "cold" seems to produce either bad outlines or, worse, only a blank piece of paper and a deep sense of guilt.

For something under a page or so, don't worry about an outline at all. It probably isn't necessary. For something longer—even just slightly longer—an outline may be helpful. Here's what I recommend:

- If you have excellent control of your content at the start, try making an outline. Don't worry about those Roman numerals—just jot something down. You may want to jot down only main headings.

- If you're a little unsure of your content, try jotting down several ideas in the order you think you should cover them. Then start writing. After writing two or three paragraphs, you'll probably warm up; that is, your mind will be focused on your material—more saturated with the information you want to cover. So reassess your outline and redo it if necessary—this time perhaps in a little more detail.

- If you're very unsure of your content, try to get more information. If you must write anyway, just start writing. As you warm up, you'll focus better and be more able to make a decent outline.

So outlines—informal ones—are helpful, but you may not want to make one until you've actually started writing.

A "Recursive" Process

Researchers today believe that most writing doesn't take place in a linear order: first prewriting, then writing, then rewriting. Rather, there's lots of looping back and forth:

- Writing for a few minutes can lead to some good prewriting.
- Prewriting a new section can lead to rewriting an earlier one.
- Rewriting can take place anytime after the writing has started—and be a continuing part of the process.

From my experience, an effective writing process has lots of recursiveness. The looping back and forth isn't a sign of terminal disorganization; it's a sign that thinking is going on.

But . . . A Linear Draft

Even though your writing process may be recursive, your draft should usually be linear. That is, you should start at the beginning and work your way straight through. The other way—writing part 2 before part 1, for example—can cause problems.

Here's why. If you have a good organization, your reader will read the document in order: page 1, then page 2, then page 3. So for you to write page 3, you need to know what the reader has already seen on pages 1 and 2. It's amazing how often good writing refers to earlier material—or depends on it.

The final version of a good document is like a tapestry—all threads are important to the final design, and all threads are in the right place.

My Own Writing Process

What happens on a typical writing project—something two or three pages long? Or even book length? What would be a good way to write that document?

We all have our special techniques, but here's what normally happens when I write:

1. I fool myself into believing I'm actually ready to write, so I start in.
2. I get stuck.
3. I then jot down a quick list of the main points I want to cover. If I can think of any subpoints, I put them in, too.
4. I arrange those points in the best order.
5. I start writing again.
6. If I find that I'm not following my original outline, I don't worry: my ideas while I'm actually writing are probably

much better than my ideas beforehand. Actually writing saturates my mind with the content, giving me a better sense of what I need to say.

7. I rarely get stuck again, but if I do, I re-outline (briefly).
8. I write quickly, with no thought for typos or other errors.
9. But I stop *immediately* if the content or organization isn't working. After all, what comes before is crucial to what comes after, so I must get the content and organization right. Otherwise, I'm wasting my time because I know I'll have to rewrite significantly.
10. When I finish writing, I read and revise immediately.
11. I then set the writing aside for awhile—even a few minutes helps disconnect my mind from the particular words on the paper.
12. Then I reread and revise, looking not just for errors but for the important matters this book covers (style, layout, etc.). Throughout, I ask these questions: "Will my reader understand?" and "Have I made my points the best way possible?"
13. Then I show the writing to someone else for feedback. I try to "lean toward" their suggestions rather than away from them. But I realize that I am the one most responsible for the content *and* most engaged with it, so I take "my" advice before theirs.
14. I watch reruns of *Cheers* on television.

Frankly, I follow that process much of the time I write. It works for me.

Normally I write about 5 pages or so at a sitting. Later I'll read and revise those pages before starting a new section. That way I'm familiar with what I've just written before starting the writing again; also, I'll have fairly polished pages as I move along.

What If There's Not Enough Time?

You may not always have time to do all that. Well, the more

comfortable you are with plain English, the faster and better you will be able to write.

Still, sometimes you can't put your writing aside. True. And sometimes you can't show your writing to someone else. True. But lots of times you *can*—and *should*.

Especially for those "career" projects that come up once or twice a year, you should build in the opportunity for these two feedback steps—feedback from someone else and feedback from yourself (after getting away from the writing for a while).

What's the Role of the Computer?

Can the computer (or other word processor) help with the writing process?

YES!

The computer is the greatest breakthrough in writing since the quill pen. It can *revolutionize* the speed and ease of getting words on paper, and the words will be better, too. Much better.

In fact, I'll go out on a limb: *you'll never be as good a writer without a computer as you can be with one*. It's that simple. Ask anyone who uses a computer for writing.

I'm not saying you can't be a superb writer without a computer. You certainly can be. Mark Twain, as I recall, didn't have a Macintosh in his study. But even Mark Twain could have been better. Just try some of his lesser novels: *Life on the Mississippi* could have benefited from a few "block deletions."

Isn't the Computer for Secretaries?

The computer as a tool for secretaries? Absolutely. It replaces the typewriter on the secretary's desk.

But it also replaces *the yellow legal pad* on the executive's desk. Just because the computer looks like a typewriter doesn't mean that's all it is. It's not just a powerful tool for recording words in a readable typeface. It's also a powerful tool for creating those words. And for rewriting them.

It looks like a typewriter. But it's much more.

How Can the Computer Help with the First Draft?

Do you ever have the sense you can think more quickly than you can get the words on paper? That's the way I used to feel when I wrote my drafts with pen and paper. As a result, I constantly lost sight of my main point and the overall flow of the document.

Now, using a computer to write my first draft, I feel as though I am recording my words at about the speed I'm thinking them. I feel as if I'm simply "talking into the computer"—through the keyboard. The result is a much more polished first draft.

Some of you may believe you can't type your first drafts into a computer because you're not good typists. On a computer, you don't have to be a good typist. First, you can look at the keyboard as you type (why look anyplace else?); second, you don't have to worry about errors because they're easy to fix later.

If you can't type at all, you should learn—the small time you invest will serve you the rest of your life. And there are computer programs that make learning to type easy.

So one important reason to use a computer for your first draft is that you'll keep the flow of your ideas in mind better. A second reason has to do with the recursiveness I mentioned earlier—the notion that writing and rewriting take place together.

If, for example, you're using pen and paper (or typewriter) and think your organization and content aren't working, you're reluctant to go back and rewrite—hard to do and messy. With a computer such revisions are a snap. You don't even hesitate to make the fixes that straighten out the entire direction of the document you're writing.

That may be the most important reason to write your first draft at a computer.

How Can the Computer Help with Rewriting?

So the computer is great in the writing stage. How useful is it for rewriting? Again, it's invaluable.

Let me illustrate with a brief story. I had a co-author on my first book, which we wrote with pen and paper. Naturally, we read each other's chapters, and then we'd meet to discuss what we'd found. Those sessions were not always pleasant. I hated to make changes the other author suggested—the revision process was time consuming, lengthy, and difficult. And he hated to make the changes I suggested.

As a result, we both fought for the *status quo*: what we had written seemed perfectly all right to us, so why should we change it? Deep down, though, we knew the other person was right. We just didn't want to go through that painful process of revision.

With a computer, that revising process is almost fun. It's easy to do. Spelling checkers take care of most spelling problems (and grammar checkers, as they become more sophisticated, will soon help with grammar). The result is a much more polished document. Think how easy layout, for example, is to change with a computer.

You can see why I hate to work with writers who do their work in pen or on a typewriter. I know they are handicapped from the start just by their physical method of getting words on paper. They will have to work much harder, and they still won't do as good a job as if they were using a computer.

So I'll stay out on that limb: *you'll never be as good a writer without a computer as you can be with one.*

Tips on Writing Quickly and Well

In summary, here are some general tips that may help you improve your writing process:

General Tips on the Writing Process

1. Use a computer.
2. Imagine you're actually talking to your reader.
3. For very short documents (a page or less), don't bother with outlines.
4. For longer documents, make informal outlines.
5. Start at the beginning of your document and work straight through to the end.
6. Don't worry about punctuation and spelling during your first draft.
7. Do worry about content and organization during your first draft.
8. Set your writing aside for a while to get some distance from it.
9. Show your writing to someone else.

CHAPTER 12

Supervising Writers:
Getting the Most from
Your People

I know that not everybody who reads this book is a supervisor. But most people either are or hope to be some day. So if you're a supervisor now, this chapter is for you. And if you're not one yet? Well, this chapter is what I would tell your boss.

So . . . for supervisors—present and future: Do you ever get frustrated by the writing your people do? If so, you're among the vast majority of supervisors.

Some people just don't understand the English language very well; most people, however, write "that way"—bureaucratically—because they believe they have to. They think that's the kind of writing *you want*: stilted, overly formal, passive, and "impressive."

After all, if you ever wrote in the bureaucratic style, didn't you write that way because you felt "that's what the boss wants"?

So what can you do to improve the writing of your people, to help them understand—and apply—the principles of plain English? Here are a few tips:

Get Computers for Your People

Make sure your people aren't still in the dark ages—get computers for them if at all possible. Computers aren't cheap—but they are getting cheaper. Your people will be much better writers if

114

they have easy access to a computer, a fast printer, and straight-forward word processing software.

Tell Your People What You Want

Remember in school when you got a paper back with red marks all over it and a comment like this: "Sentences must never begin with *and* or *but*. Don't start sentences that way in my class!" Don't you wish the teacher had told you that *before* you handed in the paper?

The same thing happens when your people write for you—if you haven't told them what you want. In fact, I suggest you tell your people in a memo that you want plain English. Tell them to write the way they talk, use pronouns, use headings, use contractions—everything. And let your memo illustrate those techniques. Then people will see the new style in action—with your signature on it.

You can use the memo time and again as you move on to new positions or as new people come to work for you. In fact, I've worked with organizations where the boss's memo on writing was one of the first pieces of paper a new employee received.

Show Them Examples of Good Writing

While examples of bad writing are all over the place, examples of good writing are sometimes hard to find. But when you have such an example, you have gold. People can do an amazing job following a good example: "Oh, *that's* what you want!"

When a good example *does* cross your desk, by all means send it to all your writers—and then congratulate the person who wrote it.

When a good example does *not* ever cross your desk, then you need to take a harder step. You need to create a good example. You can do that two ways:

- You can write the example yourself.
- You can get a good writer to write one for you.

The effort, believe me, is worth it. And if you can't find a good example from your people's writing, the effort is *especially* necessary—and *especially* worth it.

Tell Them When They Write Well for You—Or Badly

I know: you don't have time to give feedback to your writers. One reason you don't have time may be that you're dealing with too much of their bad writing. They'll keep turning it out, though, unless you intervene. Make an effort at least once to give detailed feedback to each writer.

Don't forget to tell them what they're doing right. If you don't give them reinforcement, they may never know what you like and may well change to something worse.

In Summary . . .

Good writing is worth the effort—effort from you and from your people. Think about the struggle poor writers go through just trying to get words on paper. Think about the communication that gets lost.

The simple techniques in this book—on style, organization, and layout—can make all the difference to writers, readers, supervisors.

So push for plain English at work. It's the new way to write.

APPENDIX

Simpler Words and Phrases

Bureaucratic	Better	Bureaucratic	Better
accompany	go with	facilitate	help
accomplish	do	failed to	didn't
advise	tell, recommend	forward	send
afford an opportunity	let	furnish	send
anticipate	expect	furthermore	also
approximately	about	has the capability	can
ascertain	find out	however	but
assist	help	identical	same
attached herewith is	here's	implement	carry out, do
at the present time	now	in addition	also
benefit	help	in an effort to	to
close proximity	near	inasmuch as	since
commence	begin	inception	start
complete	fill out	incumbent upon	must
conclude	end	indicate	show
concur	agree	initial	first
cooperate	help	initiate	start
deem	think	in lieu of	instead of
demonstrate	show, prove	insufficient	not enough
desire	want	in the event that	if
determine	find out	in the near future	soon
disclose	show	legislation	law
effect	make	limited number	few
elect	choose	locate	find
endeavor	try	location	place
ensue	follow	maintain	keep, support
ensure	make sure	modify	change
exhibit	show	monitor	check, watch
experience	have	negative	no

Bureaucratic	Better	Bureaucratic	Better
notify	let me know	state	say
numerous	many, most	submit	send
observe	see	subsequent	later, next
obtain	get	sufficient	enough
permit	let	supply	send
personnel	people	terminate	stop
presently	now	therefore	so
prior to	before	this office	we, us
provided that	if	time period	time
purchase	buy	transmit	send
relating to	about, on	transpire	happen
request	ask	until such time as	until
require	need	utilization	use
residence	home	utilize	use
retain	keep	viable	workable
reveal	show	whereas	since
review	check, go over	witnessed	saw

Index